Financing Quality Education For All
The Funding Methods of Compulsory and Special Needs Education

Financing Quality Education For All

*The Funding Methods of Compulsory and
Special Needs Education*

Kristof De Witte, Vitezslav Titl, Oliver Holz and Mike Smet

LEUVEN UNIVERSITY PRESS

The authors acknowledge financial support of the government of the German-speaking Community of Belgium, Steunpunt Onderwijsonderzoek (SONO) of the Flemish Ministry of Education, and KU Leuven Fund for Fair Open Access. The views expressed in this publication are the sole responsibility of the authors and do not necessarily reflect the views of the German-speaking Community of Belgium or the Flemish government.

Published in 2019 by Leuven University Press / Presses Universitaires de Louvain / Universitaire Pers Leuven. Minderbroedersstraat 4, B-3000 Leuven (Belgium).

© Kristof De Witte, Vitezslav Titl, Oliver Holz and Mike Smet, 2019
This book is published under a Creative Commons Attribution Non-Commercial Non-Derivative 4.0 Licence.

Further details about Creative Commons licenses are available at http://creativecommons.org/licenses/
Attribution should include the following information:
Kristof De Witte, Vitezslav Titl, Oliver Holz and Mike Smet, *Financing Quality Education For All: The Funding Methods of Compulsory and Special Needs Education*. Leuven, Leuven University Press. (CC BY-NC-ND 4.0)

ISBN 978 94 6270 191 5 (Paperback)
ISBN 978 94 6166 300 9 (ePDF)
ISBN 978 94 6166 301 6 (ePUB)
https://doi.org/10.11116/9789461663009
D/2019/1869/33
NUR: 805

Layout: Crius
Cover design: Frederik Danko
Cover illustration:

Contents

List of Figures 9

List of Tables 11

Chapter 1. Introduction 13

Chapter 2. The choice of countries and regions 19
- 2.1 British Columbia 22
- 2.2 Estonia 22
- 2.3 Finland 23
- 2.4 Flanders 23
- 2.5 Massachusetts 23

Chapter 3. Overview of education systems 25
- 3.1 British Columbia 25
  - Expenditure on education 26
  - Approach to special needs students and language minorities 27
  - The autonomy and providers of education 29
- 3.2 Estonia 29
  - Expenditure on education 30
  - Approach to special needs students and language minorities 30
  - The autonomy and providers of education 32
- 3.3 Finland 32
  - Expenditure on education 32
  - Approach to special needs students and language minorities 33
  - The autonomy and providers of education 35
- 3.4 Flanders 35
  - Expenditure on education 36
  - Approach to special needs students and language minorities 36
  - Autonomy and providers of education 37
- 3.5 Massachusetts 38
  - Expenditure on education 38
  - Approach to special needs students and language minorities 39
  - Autonomy and providers of education 40

Chapter 4. Funding formulas 41
4.1 British Columbia 41
Primary schools 42
An example a primary school budget in the district of Mission 47
Secondary schools 49
An example of a secondary school budget in the district of Mission 52
Support for special needs students 53
A case study on special needs funding in the district of Mission 54
A case-study of the funding formula in the district of Mission 54
Summary of the education funding system in British Columbia and the district of Mission 58
4.2 Estonia 59
Primary schools 60
An example of a primary school budget in Estonia 66
Secondary schools 67
An example of a secondary school budget in Estonia 71
Special needs schools 71
An example of a an additional funding calculation for special needs students in Estonia 72
Summary of the Estonian education funding system 73
4.3 Finland 74
Primary schools 75
An example of a primary school in a municipality in Finland 76
Secondary schools 76
An example of a secondary school in a municipality in Finland 80
Special needs schools 80
The case of the municipality of Hanko 81
An example of a school in a municipality in Finland 82
Summary of the Finnish education funding system 82
4.4 Flanders 83
Primary schools 84
An example of a primary school board budget in Flanders 91
Secondary schools 93
An example of a secondary school board budget in Flanders 103
Special needs education 105
An example of the budget of a school with special needs students in Flanders 111
Summary of the Flemish education funding system 114

4.5	Massachusetts	115
	The mechanism behind the formula	116
	The calculation of allocations	117
	An example of a primary school district budget in Massachusetts	119
	Required local contribution calculation	124
	Filling the gap with Chapter 70 education aid	124
	An example of a secondary school district budget in Massachusetts	124
	Effective funding per student	125
	Funding outside the main formula	126
	Summary of the education funding in Massachusetts	127

Chapter 5. Conclusions   129
Summary of the funding formulas in the selected regions and countries   129
Discussion   131

Appendix   139

List of primary sources   153
British Columbia   153
Estonia   153
Finland   154
Flanders   154
Massachusetts   155

References   157

List of Figures

Figure 1: Performance in science on PISA 2006-2015.   20
Figure 2: Simplified diagram of the main determinants of total allocation to school districts in British Columbia.   59
Figure 3: Secondary school population (the number of students in thousands is on the vertical axes) in Estonia.   60
Figure 4: Flow of funding from Estonian municipalities to primary and secondary schools.   65
Figure 5: Simplified diagram of the main components of total allocation to municipalities in Estonia.   74
Figure 6: The organizer specific unit price multiplier.   78
Figure 7: Simplified diagram of the main sources allocated to schools in Finland.   83
Figure 8: Simplified diagram of the main components of total allocation to primary school boards in Flanders.   115
Figure 9: Comparison of schools per pupil spending in 2010 in two sample districts.   125
Figure 10: Comparison of Massachusetts' foundation budgets rates in 2016.   126
Figure 11: Simplified diagram of the main components of total allocation to school districts in Massachusetts.   127
Figure 12: Structure of education system in Canada.   147
Figure 13: Structure of the education system in Estonia.   148
Figure 14: Structure of the education system in Finland.   149
Figure 15: Structure of the education system in Flanders.   150
Figure 16: Structure of the education system in the USA.   151

List of Tables

Table 1: Performance in science on PISA 2015.   15
Table 2: Levels of special needs in British Columbia.   28
Table 3: Calculation of funding of Deroche Elementary School.   49
Table 4: Calculation of per student funding.   62
Table 5: Additional funding for small classes.   62
Table 6: Funding for school directors and deputies.   63
Table 7: Funding of schools with students in grades 1-9.   68
Table 8: Calculation of per student funding.   69
Table 9: Coefficients for special needs students.   72
Table 10: Vocational education funding model.   78
Table 11: The unit prices per training sectors   79
Table 12: Allocations to a Flemish community school board.   93
Table 13: Additional points for specials students integrated in mainstream education.   105
Table 14: Targets numbers for different types of disabilities.   110
Table 15: Allocations to a Flemish community school board.   113
Table 16: Costs rates for primary education in Massachusetts, amounts are per pupil in 2017/18.   118
Table 17: Overview of pupil expenditures by major functional categories in North Brookfield.   120
Table 18: Costs rates for secondary education in Massachusetts, amounts are per pupil in 2017/18.   122
Table 19: Spending on education in the chosen regions and countries, the share of the young is reported as of 2014.   139
Table 20: Indices of school responsibilities for resource allocation and over curricula and assessments as measures of school autonomy countries.   139
Table 21: Overview of funding types and their characteristics in the chosen regions and countries.   140
Table 22: Shares of special needs students in 2016/2017 in the chosen regions and countries.   141

Chapter 1
Introduction

Countries around the world attempt to increase the human capital of their citizens. Currently, education constitutes a large share of the economy in developed countries. The average expenditure on primary and secondary education institutions is about 3.5% of GDP in OECD countries (OECD, 2016). Moreover, investment in education has large implications for economic development, democratic institutions as well as overall wellbeing. This makes the choice of a funding system very important for any country. Nevertheless, the academic literature does not (yet) provide a clear consensus and guidance on which system leads to the best educational outcomes. Even in cases where the literature provides a clearer picture, it shows that different funding systems lead to optimal outcomes under very different circumstances. For instance, school autonomy is positively associated with educational outcomes in developed countries; however, the relationship is negative in developing countries (Hanushek et al. 2013). Another example can be class size – the size seems to be a relevant variable only in countries with poorer teacher quality (Hanushek and Woessmann, 2017). Furthermore, it is obvious that different countries face different challenges in terms of current educational levels, teachers' training and abilities, language and geographical challenges and the like. Various educational systems also pursue different goals. Thus, it is not surprising that funding systems differ tremendously across countries and also across the best performing countries.

In this book, we discuss the funding formulas for compulsory and special needs education for chosen well-performing countries and regions on international tests such as the Programme for International Student Assessment (PISA), which is a worldwide study by the Organization for Economic Co-Operation and Development (OECD) of 15-year-old pupils' scholastic performance in mathematics, science, reading and financial literacy. We thus extend and update the books of Ross & Levačić (1999), which focuses on methods of resource allocation to education in European countries, and of Verstegen (2015), which focuses on methods of resource allocation to education in the United States. There is also a recent book by Baker (2018) on the funding of U.S. schools. We do not simply update their work and cover additional countries, but we extend their work by discussing also *(i)* recent reforms in education finance, and *(ii)* the methods of allocating funding to students with special needs. Furthermore, by studying the funding system in the best performing countries, we attempt to identify characteristics that are associated with best outcomes and the characteristics that are ideal to pursue particular goals such as equity or efficiency. For the selected countries and regions, we thus describe how the school resources are allocated and discuss whether the funding system was designed to pursue specific goals. The funding of primary, secondary and special needs education is covered. Finally, we would like to point out that we do not attempt to develop an analytical framework for how to generally assess funding systems. For such an analytical framework with emphasis on equity and equality, please see, for example, BenDavid-Hadar (2018).

We consider the following countries and regions: Estonia (position 3 in science; see Table 1 that presents the 2015 PISA results for science – the area of focus in the latest PISA report[1]), Finland (position 5), the state of Massachusetts (position 7), the Canadian province of British Columbia (position 8) and the Flemish Community of Belgium (position 16). All the chosen regions have relatively decentralized systems of funding or they are examples of a federal state in a decentralized system (such as Massachusetts and British Columbia). As seen in Table 1, the differences in performance are great even among the best performing states. Given that 40 PISA points correspond to about 1 school year's difference (OECD, 2016), we see that Estonian pupils are more than about half a school year ahead of the average Flemish students.

The results of these large-scale international tests of student achievement (such as the abovementioned PISA or TIMSS,[2] PIRLS[3] and TALIS[4]) suggest that the variation in scholastic assessment within and between countries is large. Traditionally, high performance in international tests was considered to come at the cost of a wider distribution around the average test score. Economists refer to the trade-off between equity and efficiency in outcomes (Okun, 1975).

McGrath (1993) defines equity or equality of opportunity as "*a means of ensuring that as much equality as possible is built into in the provision of educational*

---

1   The focus area of the PISA tests changes every three years.
2   The Trends in International Mathematics and Science Study (TIMSS) is a series of international assessments organized by the International Association for the Evaluation of Educational Achievement.
3   The Progress in International Reading Literacy Study (PIRLS) is an international study among fourth graders organized also by the International Association for the Evaluation of Educational Achievement.
4   The Teaching And Learning International Survey (TALIS) is an international evaluation of the conditions of teaching and learning organized by the OECD.

Jurisdiction	Average	Standard Error
Singapore	556	(1,2)
Canada: British Columbia	**539**	**(4,3)**
Japan	538	(3,0)
Estonia	**534**	**(2,1)**
Chinese Taipei	532	(2,7)
Finland	**531**	**(2,4)**
United States: Massachusetts	**529**	**(6,6)**
Macao (China)	529	(1,1)
Canada	**528**	**(2,1)**
Viet Nam	525	(3,9)
Hong Kong (China)	523	(2,5)
Spain: Castile and Leon	519	(3,5)
B-S-J-G (China)	518	(4,6)
Korea	516	(3,1)
Spain: Madrid	516	(3,5)
Belgium: Flemish Community	**515**	**(2,6)**
New Zealand	513	(2,4)
Slovenia	513	(1,3)
Spain: Navarre	512	(4,1)
Spain: Galicia	512	(3,1)
Australia	510	(1,5)
United Kingdom	509	(2,6)
Germany	509	(2,7)
Netherlands	509	(2,3)
Spain: Aragon	508	(4,6)
Switzerland	506	(2,9)
Spain: Catalonia	504	(4,7)
Ireland	503	(2,4)
United States: North Carolina	502	(4,9)
Belgium	502	(2,3)

Table 1: Performance in science on PISA 2015; note: The countries in bold are analyzed in this book; source: OECD (2017) and Council of Ministers of Education, Canada (2016).

services and as much fairness as is administratively feasible is applied to sharing the taxation burden for education among the general citizenry" (p. 1). Policies that aim at increasing equity can focus both at increasing the capacity of educational services for people who receive relatively little education and at reducing the cost for people that are carrying a larger tax burden. As students differ in observed (e.g., parental education, socio-economic status, race, gender) and unobserved (e.g. effort, ability) characteristics (Alexander, 2004; Espinoza, 2007), one can define equity from two perspectives. 'Horizontal equity' indicates that schools with comparable characteristics should receive similar resources. 'Vertical equity' implies that schools with higher costs due to different conditions and student characteristics should receive more funding (Toutkoushian and Michael, 2007). To *"ensure inclusive and equitable quality education and promote lifelong learning opportunities for all"*[5] is also one of the sustainable development goals defined by the United Nations. In this book, we discuss whether the studied funding systems achieve equality of opportunities which, furthermore, highlights the importance of our conclusions for policy makers in order to achieve these goals.

A second part of the trade-off is 'efficiency', which refers to achieving the highest educational outcomes at the lowest cost. "On the one hand, there is a basic belief that efficiency is a good and worthy goal as inefficiencies correspond to wasted resources. On the other hand, there is sense of worry that efforts to improve efficiency will ultimately undermine what lies at the heart of high-quality education. Part of the difficulty stems from a misunderstanding about the meaning of efficiency. The notion of efficiency is a disarmingly simple idea that presupposes that some inputs are transformed into outcomes in the process of the formation of human capital. One can think in terms of ingredients, inputs or resources that are transformed into results, output or outcomes. For example, in an educational setting, a teacher and the school inputs can be thought of as an ingredient (even though teaching and school inputs are an important part of the actual transformation process) and the academic attainments of students can be viewed as an outcome. The concept of efficiency is then related to a moral imperative to obtain more desired results and outcomes from fewer resources and ingredients. Efficiency needs to be thought of as a matter of degree. Efficiency is not a 'yes' or 'no' objective. It is instead better thought of in relative or comparative terms. The public impact of the international evaluation of the school systems such as the PISA tests is a clear demonstration of the importance that public opinion attaches to the notion of efficiency of the school system (relative to other school systems). The quest for greater efficiency is never over, and this sense of a never-ending quest is one source of the generalized sense of anxiety that tends to surround the efficiency concept. Standardized tests of various kinds have been relied upon as measures of the outcomes of schooling and have been criticized on different grounds" (De Witte and Hindriks, 2010).

While most educational interventions aim solely to increase equity or efficiency, they often have an effect on each other. The historic trade-off between

---

5   See https://unstats.un.org/sdgs/report/2017/goal-04/. Note also that the countries examined (Finland, Canada, Belgium, the US, and Estonia) signed these policy goals.

equity and efficiency (Okun, 1975) is nowadays heavily criticized (King Rice, 2004; Minter and Hoxby, 1996; Freeman et al., 2010; Wößmann, 2008). These authors argue that by adopting a well-designed school funding system countries and regions might succeed in obtaining high student achievement scores for the average, the above average and the least advantaged students.

To define the basic terms used throughout the book, we first briefly describe what we mean by primary, secondary and special education in the respective countries and regions. The structure of primary education systems differs across the selected regions. In British Columbia, primary education corresponds to elementary school in grades 1 to 7 (ages from 6 to 12). In Estonia, it is so-called "Basic education" in grades 1 to 9 (ages from 7 to 16); the same system is in place in Finland. The Flemish "basic education" consists of optional pre-school and six years of mandatory primary education from the age of 6. In Massachusetts, primary education is part of the K-12 education system and takes place in so-called elementary schools usually until grade 8.

Also the structure of secondary education systems differs across the countries and regions. In British Columbia, students in the ages from 12 to 18 attend secondary education (lower secondary 7th to 9th grade and upper secondary 10th to 12th grade). The Estonian system is similar; lower secondary education is provided (in the third stage of so-called basic schools) in grades 7 to 9 and at upper secondary schools for 3 more years up to 12th grade. Secondary education in Finland consists of general upper secondary schools and vocational schools attended from the age of 16 to 19. There are 4 different tracks of secondary education in Flanders which are attended by students at the age of 12 to 18 years. Finally in the state of Massachusetts, students attend secondary education within the so-called K-12 framework from the 9th to the 12th grade.

The structure and the whole system of special needs education is more complicated and largely disharmonized. There is neither a common European definition of special needs education nor a harmonized system of classification for special needs and learning difficulties. This is underlined by significant differences in the labels used across European countries to classify children with special education needs (European Commission, 2013). According to the Network of Experts in Social Sciences of Education and Training, we can distinguish so-called normative and non-normative difficulties of special needs students. The former group includes physical and sensory difficulties. Note that this makes normative difficulties relatively easy to identify and assess since there is broad agreement on what normal functioning means. The latter group includes difficulties such as social, emotional and behavioral difficulties or learning difficulties (such as dyslexia). Non-normative difficulties normally account for the majority of children identified as having special needs (European Commission, 2013).

One of the concepts of supporting special needs education is inclusive education defined by Booth (2000) as *"the process of increasing participation and decreasing exclusion from the culture, curriculum and community of mainstream schools"*. The core idea and the ultimate goal are to ensure that students with special needs have equal educational opportunities alongside their peers in mainstream education (European Commission, 2013). In 2009 Belgium ratified the UN Convention on the Rights of Persons with Disabilities. Article 24 of this Convention states that *"States Parties shall ensure an inclusive education system at all levels and lifelong learning [...] Persons with disabilities are not excluded from the general education system on the basis of disability, and that children with disabilities are not excluded from free and compulsory primary education, or from secondary education, on the basis of disability"* (United Nations, 2006). This Convention puts pressure on countries to reform current special needs education systems toward a more inclusive system. In this book, we attempt to describe the various approaches to and definitions of special needs students and provide a detailed description of the funding of education for such students.

The structure of the remainder of this book is as follows. In the following chapter, we discuss the choice of countries and regions. In Chapter 3, we describe the education systems in the chosen regions and their approach to special needs students. The funding formulas are then comprehensively described in Chapter 4. By showing specific cases of school budgets, we provide detailed and concrete insights into how the funding system in a country works. Chapter 5 provides a concluding discussion.

Chapter 2
The choice of countries and regions

Some countries succeed in systematically outperforming others in terms of their educational attainments. The regions and countries studied in this book are selected based on results in the OECD PISA tests. These tests were launched in 2000 by the OECD as a triennial survey of 15-year-old students around the world. The PISA surveys assess the extent to which 15-year-old students have acquired knowledge and skills in science, reading, mathematics and collaborative problem solving (OECD, 2016).

The choice of the target population (15-year-olds) may be problematic, as in some countries such as Mexico or Turkey enrolment in this age is below 60 percent which makes the PISA tests' outcomes not very informative about the whole of the education systems in these countries. Next to this participation bias, in certain countries, education is compulsory beyond the age of 15, meaning that some abilities of abstract reasoning are still in development at the time when the tests are taken. Therefore, the PISA tests may systematically underestimate the abilities of students in such countries. Furthermore, tests taken in different moments/ages might result in different outcomes (OECD, 2016; Wuttke, 2007).

In 2015, the area of focus of the PISA tests was science and about 540,000 (out of the population of approximately 29 million 15-year-olds in the schools) students coming from 72 countries were assessed. The best performing countries (Canada, Finland, Estonia, Japan, or Singapore) score about 520-560 points in science while the lowest performing (Algeria, Dominican Republic or Kosovo). score only about 330-380 points. To understand the extent of the difference in performance, it is good to point out that 40 points difference in scores is the equivalent of approximately one year of schooling (OECD, 2014 and 2016).

All the studied regions[6] and countries in this book perform very strongly in PISA tests – specifically in science, which is the focus of the last OECD study. Figure 1 presents a comparison of the results in the chosen regions in the period from 2006 to 2015 and it also reveals regional differences. We observe that there is a decreasing trend in performance for all selected countries between 2006 and 2015 except for Canada and Estonia.

---

6   The regions that were chosen can be seen as countries as they have their own systems of education funding.

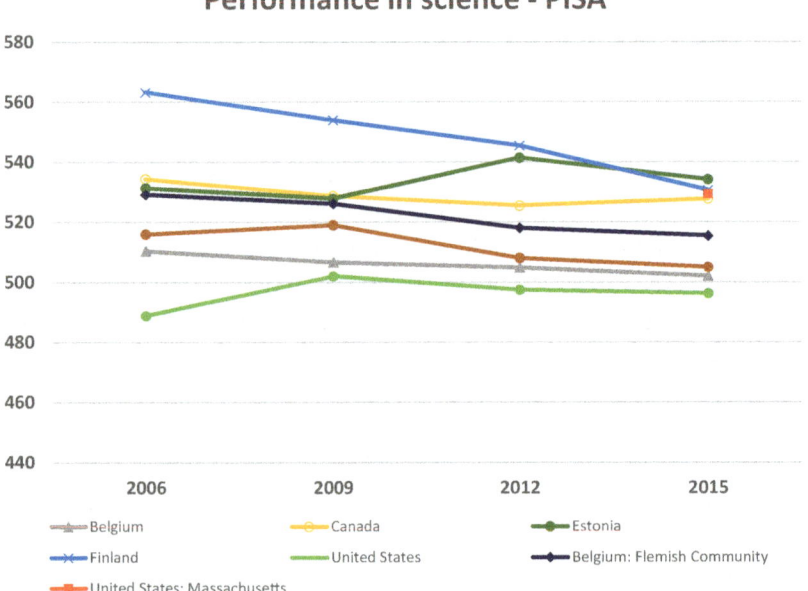

Figure 1: Performance in science on PISA 2006-2015. Note that standard deviations are presented in Table 1; source: own presentation from OECD data.

Canada ranks at position 8 in science in the test. And specifically British Columbia performs well above the OECD average in PISA tests, having the average score of 539 (see the comparison of all chosen regions in Figure 1). This is the highest score worldwide after Singapore, Quebec, and Alberta (The Council of Ministers of Education, Canada, 2016). The Canadian system shows overall very high levels of equity (De Witte and Hindriks, 2017). The impact of socio-economic status on student performance in mathematics is lower than the OECD average and students from an immigrant background perform similarly to their peers (OECD, 2015; De Witte and Hindriks, 2017).

Estonia ranks almost as highly as British Columbia and better than Canada or Finland, overall at position 3 in science when only countries are ranked. According to the OECD (2015a), Estonia generally promotes equity in the education system and the performance gap between students with a lower socio-economic background is lower than the OECD average in PISA 2012. The rate of secondary education attainment is among the highest among OECD countries as well as the proportion of adults holding a tertiary degree which shows high accessibility of education in Estonia (Santiago et al., 2016).

Finland ranks 5 among the tested countries and shows high levels of equity. However, it seems that in Finland students' background and gender matter. Both boys and students with immigrant background are at higher risk of lower performance. According to PISA 2009 results in reading, boys scored 55 points fewer than girls (compared to the OECD average of 39 points). On the other hand, there is a large percentage of top performers and a small proportion of poor performers is lower than the OECD average. The impact of socio-economic status is also generally lower than the average among OECD countries. However, since 2000, the impact of socio-economic background has been increasing.

The state of Massachusetts (position 7) strongly outperforms other American states. From the statistical point of view, only Singapore (with a score of 556 points) performs in science significantly better than Massachusetts. Similarly, students in Massachusetts (with the score of 527 points) perform above the OECD and United States averages in reading. However, in mathematics, the United States as well as Massachusetts score below the OECD average. The score of the Massachusetts' students in mathematics is close to the OECD average.

Another signal about the quality of the education system in Massachusetts is that the average science performance declined between 2012 and 2015 across OECD countries. But in Massachusetts, the average science scores in 2012 and 2015 do not significantly differ (OECD, 2016c). On the other hand, the performance among students varies a lot. The variation in Massachusetts' student performance in science (14 percent) is significantly higher than in Estonia, Finland or Canada (where the variation is less than 10 percent). The difference is attributed to differences in students' socio-economic status, which explains about 11 percent of this variation according to OECD (2015d). This suggests that the level of equity in education is lower than in the aforementioned countries.

Across OECD countries, socio-economically advantaged students perform better than disadvantaged students (on average by 40 points which is equivalent to more than one year of schooling). The share of immigrants who are in the U.S. and are more likely to come from a disadvantaged background than the rest of the population is lower in Massachusetts than in the whole of the U.S. And after accounting for socio-economic status students, the differences in performance between the immigrant and non-immigrant population is no longer significant (OECDc, 2016).

Finally, in general, according to the OECD (2016), education systems that give school principals responsibility for school governance outperform other education system in science. This positive association[7] becomes even

---

7   Please note that this does mean that there is a causal relation between the responsibility given to school principals and the educational outcomes.

stronger in countries where mandatory standardized tests of students take place regularly. The performance of the chosen regions reassures us about this relationship as most of these high performing countries give large autonomy to the schools and school districts.

We discuss some particular features of the selected countries and regions next.

2.1   British Columbia

British Columbia has full responsibility for its own education funding. It is a bilingual province which aims to support English and French minority populations (OECD, 2015).

According to OECD (2015), Canada has had positive indicators on equity in recent years. And as it is a multi-cultural society with a large share of foreign-born population (almost 20 percent), it is interesting to note that native-born students and students with an immigrant background showed no statistically significant difference in performance in mathematics.

Another interesting feature of the system is the usage of supplements for unique geographic factors – specifically the small community supplement (British Columbia, Resource Management Division, 2016). We will extensively comment on this in the discussion of the funding formula as this might be a challenge faced by many policy makers.

2.2   Estonia

According to the results in PISA, Estonia has one of the strongest education systems among all OECD countries, with well above-average results (see Figure 1) (Santiago et al., 2016).

Moreover, for its size and population of 1.34 million Estonia has a large number of municipalities – 213 in 2017 (Statistics Estonia, 2017a). Although almost 70 percent of the population live in urban municipalities, over 85 percent (or 183 out of 213) of local governments – that manage, inter alia, schools – are rural. About 65 percent of the municipalities have fewer than 3,000 residents, with the smallest having as few as 105 (OECD, 2011). In the Estonian system, the smallest municipality (Piirissaare) has the responsibility to provide the same services as the largest one, Tallinn, with a population of over 407,000. This rural character and a large number of small municipalities and schools make Estonia an interesting case study.

2.3 Finland

The Finnish educational system is an example of a Nordic fully public-funded, inclusive system that traditionally performs very well in PISA rankings (for details, see Figure 1). The high level of inclusiveness and very good education outcomes make it a very interesting case study.

25 percent of schools have under 50 students and a large part of the country is rural in character. The funding system is heavily decentralized and decided by local authorities. The level of decentralization and very high performance make Finland an interesting case. We will focus on the formula for transfers to the municipalities and a case study from a chosen municipality.

2.4 Flanders

The Flemish Community of Belgium is the best performing community out of the three institutional communities of Belgium. It is particularly successful in reading skills and promoting a second language in education. In Flanders, school boards are granted funds from the central government and they then run schools while enjoying a greater level of autonomy in curriculum development.

2.5 Massachusetts

The U.S. students' performance in PISA tests remained below or close to the OECD average. However, the state of Massachusetts outperforms other American regions. From a statistical point of view, only Singapore (with a score of 556 points in science) performs significantly better than Massachusetts. Similarly, students in Massachusetts (with a score of 527 points) perform above the OECD and United States averages in reading (OECD, 2016c). We will therefore analyze this state as it constitutes a good example of a federal state/region that outperforms the rest of the country in a heavily decentralized system.

Chapter 3
Overview of education systems

As the organization of education matters in the allocation of resources, in this chapter we provide short overviews of the compulsory education systems – including both primary and secondary education – in their respective countries and regions with a focus on total expenditure on education. Furthermore, we discuss approaches to special needs students, and in appropriate cases also on the approach to language minorities (such as the Russian-speaking minority in Estonia or the Swedish-speaking minority in Finland) in the chosen regions and countries.

In the Appendix, we present a systematic comparison of levels of spending (in per capita terms as well as a share of gross domestic product (GDP)) and the shares of the young population in Table 19. This is based on the idea that higher spending on education leads to better educational outcomes (for causal evidence on this topic, see Jackson et al. 2016). The shares of the young population are presented to control for the differences in the school-age population across countries. However, as this might not a precise measure, we also include per student expenditure in PPP terms in the same table. A systematic comparison of the structures of educational systems in the chosen regions and countries is provided in Figure 12, Figure 13, Figure 14, Figure 15, and Figure 16 (in appendix).

3.1 British Columbia

In Canada, education is a provincial responsibility, and while there is some co-operation between provinces, each is independently responsible for the curriculum, teacher training and certification, laws, and funding.

In British Columbia, there are two school networks consisting of public schools that are fully funded by the provincial government and independent schools (e.g. schools with religious affiliations, private schools etc.) that are partially funded by the province. Provided that they comply with provincial regulations, i.e. they follow the British Columbia curriculum, independent schools are funded to 50 percent of the public school rate. Perhaps also due to the relatively high financial support for independent schools in the province, British Columbia had the lowest – but still very high – enrolment level in public schools at 86.8 percent in Canada (Fraser Institute, 2017).

There are approximately 1,600 public schools organized into 60 school districts and 350 independent schools. These districts vary significantly in size and population. Stikine District, for example, is geographically larger than many middle-sized European countries such as the Czech Republic or Belgium with just 200 students in it. On the other hand, there is the suburban district of Surrey, with over 75,000 students. This makes the challenges of these two districts significantly different and the funding formula thus must be designed to balance these differences.

In British Columbia, children between the ages of 6 and 12 attend elementary schools which corresponds to primary education, and pupils of the ages of 12 to 18 attend secondary education. In some districts with large numbers of students aged between 11 and 13, and where adequate facilities are available, there might also be middle schools for students of this age. In this case, students leave primary schools earlier to attend the middle schools; the length of compulsory education is not changed by this.

According to the statistics of the Ministry of Education of British Columbia (2016b), there were 641,127 students enrolled in the province in the 2016/17 academic year. This number consists of 557,630 students enrolled in public schools and 83,497 enrolled in independent schools. 371,763 of all those students were enrolled in elementary school which includes kindergarten (children at age of 5) and Grades 1 to 7 (ages from 6 to 12), and about 258,780 full-time students in secondary schools (students aged 13 to 17). The share of French Immersion students across both public and private schools was about 8.4 percent in the 2016/17 academic year (British Columbia, Ministry of Education, 2016b).

The statutory teaching hours in British Columbia are set at 22 to 23 per week in lower secondary schools. The number for primary schools was not available; this number can be taken as a lower bound as primary school teachers usually teach more hours than secondary school teachers (Jensen et al., 2016).

In the public schools of British Columbia, there were approximately 7.2 percent of students with special needs. These students attend regular classes (British Columbia, Ministry of Education, 2016b).

Expenditure on education

Expenditure on educational institutions in British Columbia was 5.7 percent of GDP in 2013, which was above the OECD average of 5.2 percent. The expenditure on primary and secondary education was 3.0 percent, which is below the OECD average of 3.5 percent (Statistics Canada, 2016b).

The figures for shares of public and private sources are not available for the province alone; therefore, we provide figures for the whole of Canada. The share of expenditure on primary education coming from public sources was 92 percent in 2013 (compared to the OECD average of 93 percent), while the share of expenditure on upper secondary education from public sources was 92 percent (compared to 87 percent, the average among OECD countries) (OECD, 2016).

Annual expenditures per student (in equivalent USD converted using PPP for GDP) on pre-primary, primary, lower secondary, and upper secondary education was 9,198, which is below the OECD average of 9,258 and the lowest of all Canadian provinces (Statistics Canada, 2016a).

Approach to special needs students and language minorities

As early as in March 1970, a Special Education Division – which was the first guide for school districts for the development of their special education programs – was created in British Columbia. A revised version of the guide from the beginning of the 1980s became more comprehensive and put stronger emphasis on the need for Individual Education Plans. Later, in response to the conclusions of the Royal Commission on Education from 1987, the School Act was revised in 1989 in order to solve the issue that special funding was received by approximately 6.2 percent of the student population even though, according to the studies, 12 percent of students had special needs. The basic premise of the new legislation was that all school-age children were entitled to an educational program, meaning that students with special needs were no more *"separated from other students in terms of defining their basic right to an educational program"* (Siegel, L. and L. Stewart, 2000, p. 9).

Currently, all school districts in British Columbia receive the so-called "Basic Allocation" which is a standard amount of money determined based on school-age pupils enrolled in a school district. This allocation already includes resources for most of the special needs students, and it is meant to support the needs of pupils who are identified *"as having learning disabilities, mild intellectual disabilities, students requiring moderate behaviour supports and students who are gifted"* (British Columbia, Ministry of Education, p.138, 2016). On top of that some pupils with special needs may require additional support and funds which are provided mainly in order to make the education system more inclusive; thus, the schools receive funds to hire additional staff, learning materials or other equipment. These funds are provided for pupils with needs in the following categories: *"physically dependent, deafblind, moderate to profound intellectual disabled, physically disabled/chronic health impaired, visually impaired, deaf/hard of hearing, autism spectrum disorder, and intensive behaviour interventions/serious mental illness"* (BC Ministry of Education, p.138, 2016). The overall goal of such additional funding is to make pupils with needs fully participating members of a class, i.e., British Columbia promotes an inclusive education system. However, as pointed out by British Columbia, Special Education Services (2016, p.2) *"...the practice of inclusion is not necessarily synonymous with full integration in regular classrooms, and goes beyond placement to include meaningful participation and the promotion of interaction with others".*

Special needs students are classified into 3 levels of so-called unique special needs and the districts receive supplements for students classified in one of the levels. These levels and the associated disabilities are presented in Table 2. The share of public school students identified as having special needs in one of these levels was 10.6 percent[8] in 2016/2017 (British Columbia, Ministry of Education, 2016b). The share has been steadily increasing in recent years. For instance in 2007/2008, the share was about 8.3 percent (British Columbia Teachers' Federation, 2012).

Level 1	Level 2	Level 3
Physically dependent (A) Deafblind (B)	Moderate to profound Intellectual disabilities (C) Physically disabled or chronic health impairment (D) Visually impairment (E) Deaf or hard of hearing impairment (F) Autism spectrum disorder (G)	Intensive behavior interventions or serious mental illness (H)

Table 2: Levels of special needs in British Columbia; source: British Columbia, Ministry of Education (2016a).

Regarding the support of language minorities, there are two kinds of French-speaking programs in public schools of British Columbia: for students who are French native speakers and for French Immersion programs. Both may begin at the beginning of elementary education. Except for these programs, there are also French-language classes as part of the regular school curriculum. These classes begin when students are 8 years old (British Columbia, Ministry of Education, 2016b).

---

8   In nominal numbers, it was 59,254 out of 557,630 enrolled in public schools.

The autonomy and providers of education

Canadian schools have, in general, less autonomy than the OECD average. This is the case in resource allocation autonomy and in responsibility for curriculum and assessment (OECD, 2016). However, as pointed out above, provinces are responsible for curriculum, funding etc.

However, in British Columbia, school districts receive lump-sum payments and have relatively large autonomy in allocating these resources to schools.

3.2 Estonia

School organization is mostly the responsibility of the municipalities in Estonia (OECD, 2015a) and the share of students in private schools is very low.

Primary education has two stages: grades 1-3 and grades 4-6. Lower secondary education is grades 7-9 and upper secondary education is grades 10-12. The schools are known as gymnasiums (in Estonian "gümnaasium") and vocational educational institutions (OECD, 2015c). Primary and lower secondary education comprises basic education for which attendance is compulsory until the age of 17 (OECD, 2015c).

There were 351 basic schools and 168 secondary schools in Estonia in the 2016/2017 academic year in which there were 135,700 full-time students enrolled in general education in public schools and 8,000 in private schools (Statistics Estonia, 2017b).

Estonia uses national exams, sample-based national tests and regular classroom assessments to assess student performance (OECD, 2015c). Such school inspections were often shown to be positively associated with students' learning outcomes (Mathew and Sammons, 2004; Luginbuhl Webbink and Wolf, 2009; McCrone et al. 2009).[9] Furthermore since 2006, schools have had to conduct self-evaluations at least once every three years.

The Estonian funding formula assumes on average 21 lessons per teacher per week.

There were 3,200 students with special needs studying in 38 general education schools (Statistics Estonia, 2017b).

---

9 It should be noted that there is also counter evidence showing the opposite effect of school inspections; however, most recent studies find positive effects.

Expenditure on education

Estonian expenditure on educational institutions was 5.2 percent of GDP in 2013 – the same as the OECD average. The expenditure on primary education was 1.5 percent, which is comparable to the average of OECD countries. The expenditure on secondary education was 1.4 percent, which is well below the OECD average of 2.1 percent (OECD, 2016, p. 209).

The share of expenditure on primary education coming from public sources was 98 percent in 2013 (compared to the OECD average of 93 percent), while the share of expenditure on lower and upper secondary education from public sources was 98 percent (compared to 93 and 87 percent, respectively).

Annual expenditure per student (in equivalent USD converted using PPP for GDP) at primary and secondary education level was 7,138 and 6,417, respectively (below the OECD average of 8,412 and 9,751, respectively).

According to Levačić (2011), there were two main influences that have impacted the costs of education provision in the last two decades. The first was a big decrease in the number of school-age children; this population has declined since the peak of 218,000 in the 1997/98 academic year by about one third to 135,700 students in 2017/18. The second factor is that less than 70 percent of the Estonian population is ethnic Estonian. About 25 percent are Russian-speaking Estonians. The municipalities are required to provide education also in a minority language, which is another factor that contributes to a decline in school and class sizes which, in turn, leads to higher per student costs.

Approach to special needs students and language minorities

Teaching of special needs students started as early as in the nineteenth century in Estonia when the first school for deaf children was founded in 1866. This continued also at the beginning of the twentieth century by the establishment of more schools for deaf, blind or moderately retarded students. The development slowed down slightly during the Soviet regime when students with moderate to severe mental disabilities were considered unteachable and sent to nursing homes. However, since the beginning of the 1990s, when the country again became independent, special education has undergone substantial changes and development. All children now have the right to be provided with education that fits their special needs (Reynolds and Fletcher-Janzen, 2007; Padrik, 2010).

Since 2004 when Estonia became a member of the European Union, the country has continued to promote inclusiveness in its education system and it has enacted ways to support weaker students and to ensure equity. Every year each student undergoes a development interview and subsequently schools are required to implement appropriate measures for the lowest achieving students. Since 2016 schools have provided school lunches, study books and learning materials for free to students in basic education. Schools are furthermore required to recruit coordinators for students with special needs, and since 2007 there has also been additional personalized support including special needs education, speech therapy, psychological assistance and social pedagogical counselling to prevent students from dropping out. Such services are more often used by rural schools than urban schools, which again helps to reduce inequality related to the place of residence (Kirss, 2011).

There are two types of special needs education: state special needs schools and municipal special needs schools. The state special needs schools – for students with disabilities such as visual, hearing or speech impairments, mobility disabilities (combined with learning special needs), intellectual disabilities and similar – receive funding allocations that are calculated based on enrolled students, and moreover the operating costs of the school are covered by the state. On the other hand, the municipal special needs schools receive their funding – through municipalities – based on the same principles as mainstream schools. The operational costs of municipal schools are covered by the municipalities. In both cases, the funding formula is designed to reflect an appropriate ratio of students per teacher that a particular student needs. This ratio is determined by the severity of the disability and the type of curriculum the student is being taught, and establishes 5 types of classes with from 1 to 12 students. In 2013/14, the share of special needs students in the school system was 4.4 percent; compared to 3.9 percent in 2007/08 (Ministry of Education and Research, 2015a). Both figures are significantly lower than in other countries.

The Estonian government committed itself to guaranteeing equal education opportunities regardless of students' ethnic origin. Consequently, it established special counselling centers in order to guarantee the quality of instruction. At the same time, Russian-language upper secondary schools have to teach subjects (with the exception of the Russian language) in Estonian. This also affects students in lower secondary education due to the overlap of the teaching staff on those two levels. In order to improve the proficiency of Russian teachers in the Estonian language; in-service courses and updated teaching materials are provided. This also aims to allow such teachers to participate in professional development activities together with Estonian-speaking teachers (OECD, 2015c).

The autonomy and providers of education

After the Basic Schools and Upper Secondary Schools Act (Estonian State Chancellery, 1993) came into force in 1993, Estonian local governments were assigned responsibility for general education and the ownership of the majority of public schools was transferred to municipalities. The Act also provided municipalities with transfers for funding of the municipality schools. Together with these changes, school principals were granted considerable autonomy which included the authority "*to hire and fire staff, negotiate working conditions and job contracts, and make decisions about school finances, education priorities and development plans for the school*" (Santiago et al., 2016). The principals are also in charge of the recruitment of teachers (Levačić, 2011).

3.3   Finland

The central government defines desired educational outcomes; however, municipalities then have great autonomy in maintaining schools in Finland. Most education providers are funded and organized by the state and municipalities (OECD, 2015b).

The educational system in Finland is compulsory from the age of 7 to 16 when students attend a nine-year comprehensive school. Schools do not in general offer any special teaching to "gifted" students as they are expected to help other students. After primary education, students can choose to attend upper secondary schools or vocational schools for 3 years.

At the end of 2016, there were 3,395 educational institutions with about 1.85 million students enrolled in Finland. Those were made up of 2,339 comprehensive schools with 532,700 students (789 of which had fewer than 100 pupils) and 75 comprehensive-school level special education schools. An interesting challenge is that the number of these schools has decreased by 24 percent in the last decade (Official Statistics of Finland, 2017a).

Finnish teachers in primary schools spend about 24 hours a week teaching. The number of teaching hours for secondary school teachers might be a bit lower and differs for lower (16-23 teaching hours) and upper (18-24) secondary subjects (Finnish National Board of Education, n.d.).

Expenditure on education

Finland's expenditure on educational institutions was 5.7 percent of GDP in 2013, i.e. above the OECD average of 5.2 percent, while the expenditure on primary education was 1.3 percent (below the average of OECD countries). The expenditure on primary education was 1.3 percent (below the average of OECD countries; OECD, 2016, p. 209) while the expenditure on secondary education was 2.6 percent, which is well above the OECD average of 2.1 percent (OECD, 2016, p. 209).

Primary and lower secondary education in Finland is solely funded from public sources (the OECD average share of funding from public resources was 93 percent for both levels), while upper secondary education was funded from public resources as to 99 percent in 2013 (the average share of expenditure from public sources among OECD countries was 87 percent) (OECD, 2016).

Annual expenditure per student (in equivalent USD converted using PPP for GDP) at primary and secondary education level was 8,519 and 10,237, respectively (slightly above the OECD average of 8,412 and 9,751 USD) (OECD, 2016).

Approach to special needs students and language minorities

In Finland, already since the 1970s, additional support in the form of 'part time special education' has been provided to anybody who had been noticed to have any kind of learning or behavioral difficulties. No special administrative decisions were needed to receive this help.

Between 2001 and 2010, there had been a steady increase in full-time special needs students who were placed in the regular classroom. The number of these full-time special education students integrated in regular classrooms increased from 15 to 30 percent within this period. As a response to this dramatic increase, a new funding formula (the Act for Amendment of Basic Education Act, enacted on August 1, 2011) was introduced in 2010. This formula is based on an estimate of a number of special needs students rather than the actual number of enrolled students, and most of the special needs students do not receive any extra funding. This was achieved by making a teacher more involved in working with the diversities in the regular classroom instead of other special support (Kirjavainen, Pulkkinen, and Jahnukainen 2014).

The Act also introduced a new tiered system for special needs education. This multi-tiered system provides the basis on which it is decided what additional support is needed for particular students. It aims to identify difficulties early on; no diagnosed disability is required in order to be eligible for help. At the same time, it promotes inclusiveness and aims to lower the number of full-time special needs students, which in turn means reducing the costs of special education (Kirjavainen, Pulkkinen, and Jahnukainen 2014).

There are 3 tiers of support for students in the Finnish system. Tier 1 (or general support) is established in order to provide good instruction for students having so-called "normal diversities" and should provide good quality basic education and general support to all student. This is in contrast with the response-to-intervention model that is common, for instance, in the United States, where more pressure on evidence-based practices and scientifically validated curricula is placed. Sahlberg (2011) argues that the different approach can be explained by the different educational standards. The variation in terms of quality of education is very small in Finland, while the quality of instruction differs a lot in the United States.

Tier 2 (or intensified support) is established for those students for whom Tier 1 intervention is not sufficient (i.e. there is no response-to-intervention at the first level) and that need *"occasional and perhaps relatively short-term additional instruction or curriculum adaptations to meet their needs"* (Vaughn and Denton 2008, p. 52). Tier 2 is estimated to cover more than 20 percent of students (Jahnukainen, 2011). At this level, more targeted interventions in smaller groups or co-teaching by specialists is employed. These special educators are a kind of jacks of all trades as they work with different kinds of students with a great variety of special needs (Kirjavainen, Pulkkinen, and Jahnukainen 2014).

Tier 3 (or special support) can be understood as *"special education where students with extraordinary needs are provided research-based instruction designed to respond to those needs"* (McLoughlin and Lewis 2008, p. 243). In the Finnish model, Tier 3 is a replacement of the earlier full-time special education, and it was assumed to cover about 5 percent of all students. It can be organized in a fully inclusive setting or in special schools (Jahnukainen, 2011; Kirjavainen, Pulkkinen, and Jahnukainen, 2014). Similarly, as in other Tiers, there was a steady decline in the number of Tier 3 students after the peak in 2010 (8.5 percent) to 7.5 percent in 2016 (Official Statistics of Finland, 2017).

In the Finnish education system, as in other Scandinavian systems since 1970s, the aim has been to equalize educational opportunities – i.e. to help the weakest students. In this setting, the help to gifted students has been seen as rather elitist. Nevertheless since 2007, Finnish government programs have mentioned fostering talent as a national goal and recognized the potential talent of gifted students as one of the main development areas of the country. However so far, such students have not received any extra funding on a national level. Currently, there are some (mostly secondary) special schools that receive private funding which offer programs for gifted students, for instance, with instruction in foreign languages or voluntary groups in which mathematics, critical thinking, IT skills etc. are taught (Tirri and Kuusisto, 2013).

The autonomy and providers of education

As argued before, a vast majority of Finnish education providers are funded by the state and local authorities. Local authorities received funding according to the formula (as presented in Chapter 4.3) and then they freely decide how to distribute the resources to different policy areas. The formula balances the proportion of population and its socio-economic status. Private education providers also receive public funding. The share of students enrolled in private primary and lower secondary education is below 5 percent and about 18 percent in upper secondary education. The funding of basic education is included in statutory government transfers to municipalities so that the authorities may decide how the resources are allocated. The funding of upper secondary education is calculated based on the number of students in schools and the unit costs per student (OECD, 2013).

3.4 Flanders

In Flanders, education is compulsory for children from the age of 6 up to the age of 18 (Informatie Vlaanderen, 2017). Compulsory education consists of primary education (6-12 years) and secondary education (12-18 years). In primary education, there are no tracks and all students enrolled in general education attend the same classes. In secondary education, a distinction is made between four tracks (general, technical, vocational and arts secondary education).

There are three education networks in Flanders, which are Community education, Municipal and provincial education, and Private-run schools. The share of privately run schools is very high at about 64.4 percent in 2012/13. In the period, there were in total 3,628 schools within these networks that cover both mainstream (2,368 primary schools and 954 secondary schools) and special schools (193 primary schools and 113 secondary special schools). In these schools (including pre-primary education) 1,127,802 students were enrolled (Nusche et al., 2015).

The number of special needs schools (9.2 percent of all schools) is high, and these schools provide education solely for special needs students, which, in turn, translates into a large total student population being educated separately from the mainstream students (5.2 percent). This is actually the highest share among the education systems in the European Union (Nusche et al., 2015).

Expenditure on education

In Belgium, expenditure on educational institutions was 5.8 percent of GDP in 2013, which is above the OECD average of 5.2 percent. Expenditure on primary education was 1.6 percent, which is comparable to the average of OECD countries and 2.8 percent on secondary education (i.e. above the OECD average of 2.1 percent) (OECD, 2016, p. 209).

Primary education in Belgium was funded as to 97 percent from public sources (the OECD average share of funding from public resources was 93 percent), while lower and upper secondary education was funded from public resources as to 96 percent in 2013 (the shares of expenditure among OECD countries from public sources were 93 and 87 percent, respectively) (OECD, 2016).

In 2016, total expenditure on primary education and preschools was almost 3.8 billion EUR in Flanders, out of which approximately half a billion EUR went to special needs schools. The average cost per student in mainstream primary education in Flanders was 4,759 EUR in 2016, for special needs students this was 17,824 EUR (Vlaamse Overheid, 2016). Secondary education had a 4.1 billion euro budget in 2016 of which 3.7 billion was spent on mainstream education and 427 million EUR on special needs students. The average cost per pupil was 8,500 and 21,000 EUR, respectively (Vlaamse Overheid, 2016).

Approach to special needs students and language minorities

In both primary and secondary education there are special schools accessible for students with disabilities. In primary education, there are 9 groups of disabilities that are recognized: mild mental handicap (type 1), moderate to severe mental handicap (2), severe emotional or behavioral issues (3), physical handicap (4), hospitalized children or children in a preventorium (5), visual handicap (6), auditory handicap (7), autism spectrum disorder without mental handicap (8) and severe learning disabilities (9). Special schools then organize education in one or more of these disability groups. A center for student counseling (CLB) can issue a certificate of enrollment that allows students to enroll in special educational institution. This advice, however, is non-binding and parents can still decide to send their children to a mainstream school (Informatie Vlaanderen, 2017b). The share of students in primary and secondary school identified as special needs students was 6.63 percent in 2012 (European Agency for Development in Special Needs Education, 2012).

In secondary education, the types of disabilities that could allow a child to enroll in special schools are the same with the exception of severe learning disabilities. Again, the CLB can write a certification of enrollment, but parents can choose to enroll their child in a mainstream school, in which case the school has to register the student at least temporarily (Informatie Vlaanderen, 2017c).

As mentioned above, a large number of students with special needs attend (separated) special schools, but not all such students do so. Until 2016/2017, they could be enrolled in integrated education (within a program called 'Geïntegreerd Onderwijs' – GON); nevertheless, this was done under the guidance and support of a special school. In 2013, the number of students enrolled in this program was 12,278. Furthermore, there has been the inclusive education project (ION) under which students with severe or moderate mental impairments can participate in mainstream education while having a modified and individualized curriculum: there were 111 students in this project in 2013.

From 2017/2018,[10] these two programs will be replaced by a new support model in primary and secondary education that will promote and support cooperation between special and mainstream schools. We describe the new model and its funding in the chapter on the Flemish funding formula for special education.

The Flemish Community does not have recognized special schools for gifted students. Nevertheless, there are some primary and secondary schools with adapted classes for gifted students (so-called kangoeroe-classes). The funding for these classes originates from the basic allocation (although it is permitted to use the teaching hours for remediation for high ability students). A class for gifted students (i.e. students with an IQ of more than 130) is thus created by grouping together all the gifted students in the school. A common practice for 'twice exceptional students' was to create learning communities where students with the same needs (e.g. autism and high abilities) were grouped. While students with autism (type 8, see before) receive additional funding, this is not the case for high ability students. This reduced the practice of similar learning communities.

Autonomy and providers of education

In Flanders, schools have to meet minimal requirements in order to receive government subsidies. This includes mainly setting out a curriculum in line with the objectives of the Community government, i.e., in principle schools can choose how to achieve the goals but they cannot choose the goals themselves. Schools

---

10   The description of the new system is available on http://data-onderwijs.vlaanderen.be/edulex/document.aspx?docid=15071.

have full autonomy in the content of optional subjects and they choose teaching methods, textbooks, grouping and assessment of pupils etc. (Hindriks, 2010).

According Nusche et al. (2015), 89 percent of the decisions regarding the organization of instruction are made by Flemish schools (and the rest by the central government). They also make 75 percent of the personnel management decisions and 71 percent of the planning and structures decisions. However, regarding resource management, they make only 50 percent of the decisions. This is also revealed in the chapter on the Flemish funding formula, because the allocations to school boards more often than in other countries are earmarked amounts (and not a lump-sum amount as is often the case in other funding systems).

3.5   Massachusetts

There were 1,854 schools[11] comprised of 1,143 elementary, 315 middle/junior high and 396 secondary schools in the Commonwealth of Massachusetts as of October 1, 2016. In those schools, 953,748 children were studying, of whom 856,760 students were attending so-called K-12 education (i.e. elementary and secondary education) and the rest were attending kindergartens and pre-kindergartens. 17.4 percent of the students were considered students with disabilities (Massachusetts Department of Elementary and Secondary Education, 2017).

Expenditure on education

Massachusetts' expenditure on K-12 education was 4.07 percent of the state's GDP in 2010. This is below the U.S. states' and OECD average of 4.31 and 5.2 percent, respectively (in 2013) (Gustafson, 2012).

The exact figures for shares of public and private sources are not available for the state alone, therefore, we provide figures for the United States of America. The share of expenditure on primary education coming from public sources was 93 percent in 2013 (the same as the OECD average), while the share of expenditure on upper secondary education from public sources was 91 percent (compared to the OECD average of 87 percent) (OECD, 2016).

Massachusetts' annual inflation-adjusted expenditure per student (in USD) at elementary and secondary education levels was 15,886 (above the OECD and U.S. states' averages) in the 2013/14 academic year (Cornman and Zhou, 2016).

---

11   This figure also includes charter schools.

Approach to special needs students and language minorities

In the United States, the major federal law regulating special needs education is the 'Individuals with Disabilities Education Act' (IDEA), previously (between 1975 and 1990) known as the 'Education for All Handicapped Children Act' (EHA). The main goal of the legislation is to ensure that students with a disability are provided with free and appropriate education that fits their special needs. In principle, the premise is to give all children the same opportunity for education.

Following the federal legislation, all children in Massachusetts with a disability that affects their educational progress have rights to obtain education that is designed to meet their special needs. Children are eligible for special education services provided that they are found to be in need of specially designed instruction to make progress and/or to access the general curriculum. Special needs education at the state level is regulated by the Massachusetts General Laws and the Code of Massachusetts Regulations (Children's Law Center of Massachusetts, 2013).

For the purpose of calculating funding allocation to the districts, Massachusetts does not classify different types of student with a disability. The funding formula assumes a fixed number of special needs students (rather than counting actual numbers) and incorporates the funding of special education into the basic allocation that is based on numbers of students in different categories and their cost rates (these reflect students' needs in terms of school funding such as administration, classroom and specialist teachers or psychological services). On top of this basic allocation, the state provides an excess cost grant to reimburse districts for additional special education expenditures (Connecticut School Finance Project, 2016).

Schools are obliged to identify and assess the children who might be eligible for special education services. A parent or any person in a care-giving position can also refer a student for an assessment. The children are then evaluated in order to provide the team of professionals who work with them with the information about whether and if so what disability the child has. The re-evaluation must be completed at least every 3 years (Children's Law Center of Massachusetts, 2013).

Children are eligible for special education services if they are aged 3 to 21 and have one of the following disabilities *"autism, developmental delay, intellectual impairment, sensory impairment (hearing, vision), neurological impairment, emotional impairment, communication impairment physical impairment, health impairment (includes ADD/ADHD) or specific learning disability".* (Children's Law Center of Massachusetts, 2013, p. 1). Furthermore in order to be eligible, they have to be, due to this disability, unable to make progress in regular education and require special instruction in order to make such progress. In 2016/2017, about 17,56 percent were identified as eligible for special education services.[12]

Lastly, in Massachusetts, there is no state-wide definition of gifted students. Districts are nevertheless allowed to identify gifted students or provide services for them. In 2010, state funding for gifted students in the form of a discretionary grant for professional development was stopped. The funding was limited to students scoring three or more standard deviations above the mean on an aptitude test and certain other requirements which were equivalent to approximately 0.125 percent of top students. The aim was mainly to help talented students from low-income backgrounds by providing, e.g., honors classes (Garland, 2009).

Autonomy and providers of education

Similarly, as in other regions and countries in this book, schools in Massachusetts do not receive the funds directly from the federal states, but there are school districts as an intermediate step (as in British Columbia). Districts have autonomy in deciding what to do with the funds they obtain. There are no specific spending or reporting requirements (Connecticut School of Finance, 2016). Moreover, schools in Massachusetts enjoy relatively large autonomy in curriculum development. The share of responsibility for the curriculum held by school principals in Massachusetts (33 percent) is larger than the average in the United States (24 percent) or the average among OECD countries (22 percent) (OECD, 2016).

---

12 In nominal terms, it was 167530/953748.

Chapter 4
Funding formulas

This chapter discusses the funding formulas for the 5 selected countries and regions. For each country, we distinguish between primary, secondary and special needs schools'/students' funding. As in all subchapters, we follow the same structure to describe the funding mechanism. First, we describe the funding formula for primary education, followed by that for secondary education and, finally, we describe the support for special needs students. In some cases, this division between primary and secondary education might be artificial as there is in fact just one funding formula; however, we keep the description of these two systems at least partially separate for the sake of consistency between chapters. The subchapter on special needs education includes students in regular classes as well as separate special needs schools. In British Columbia, Estonia, Finland and Massachusetts, we describe how the central government calculates the transfers to municipalities and we present some case studies of chosen municipalities in order to explain how the funds are then allocated to particular schools or schools districts. The funding formula in the Flemish system provides school boards with some funds that they can flexibly allocate among schools and classes (by changing school sizes or merging grades) but also with some ear-marked allocations (such as some allocations for additional lessons or on ICT).

It should be noted that a summary of the funding system, including a diagram, is presented at the end of each sub-chapter. Based on availability, we also include a (simplified) example of a primary and secondary school/ school district funding calculation at the end of each sub-chapter. Table 21 provides a systematic overview of the main characteristics of each system.

4.1 British Columbia

Primary school districts in British Columbia receive funding on a per pupil basis, while secondary school districts are funded on a per course basis. The total funding consists of so-called "Basic Allocation" (for the 2017/18 academic year, this covered about 79 percent of the total allocation), "Unique Student" (13 percent), "Unique District" (7.5 percent), and "Funding Protection / Enrolment Decline" (0.5 percent). The "Basic Allocation" is the same as for primary and secondary school students (the allocation per course is set to 1/8 of the basic allocation per eligible primary school-age full-time equivalent pupil). The secondary school funding differs mostly in some aspects of the calculation of "Unique Student" and "Unique District" allocations.

The Basic Allocation is a standard amount of money determined by the number of school-age pupils enrolled in a school district, and it includes resources to support the needs of pupils who are identified *"as having learning disabilities, mild intellectual disabilities, students requiring moderate behaviour supports and students who are gifted"* (BC Ministry of Education, p.138, 2016). The allocation recognizes needs for additional funding to support Boards of Education in providing learning assistance, speech-language pathology services, hospital homebound services, and assessment services. Regarding gifted students, a special guide has been developed for teachers on how to approach and help such students already for the 2006/2007 academic year.[13] However, the numbers of students identified as gifted have dropped dramatically from 2.5 percent in 2002/2003 to 1.1 in 2013/2014. This is often explained as a consequence of there being no extra funding for students identified as gifted (Sherlock and Skelton, 2015).

The Basic Allocation differs for (1) Standard (Regular), Continuing Education and Alternate schools and for (2) Distributed Learning.[14] For the first type of schools, districts receive 7,218 CAD in the 2016/17 academic year per eligible school-age full-time equivalent (FTE) student enrolled in the district. For the latter, the districts receive 6,030 CAD per eligible school-age full-time equivalent (FTE) student enrolled in schools and reported in the September enrolment count (British Columbia, Resource Management Division, 2016). In the remainder of this chapter we discuss the standard schools.

Primary schools

Basic Allocation
The Basic Allocation is a standard amount of money determined by the number of school-age pupils enrolled in a school district and it includes resources to support the needs of pupils who are identified *"as having learning disabilities, mild intellectual disabilities, students requiring moderate behaviour supports and students who are gifted"* (BC Ministry of Education, p.138, 2016).

The Basic Allocation per eligible school-age full-time equivalent (FTE) primary school pupil in the district was set at 7,218 CAD in the 2016/17 academic year (British Columbia, Resource Management Division, 2016).

---

13 The guide is available online at http://www2.gov.bc.ca/assets/gov/education/kindergarten-to-grade-12/teach/teaching-tools/inclusive/gifted-education.pdf [accessed on 2017/09/03].
14 The term used for distance learning in Canada.

Unique Student

On top of the Basic Allocation, some primary school pupils with special needs may require additional support and funds. There are 3 different levels of special needs support in British Columbia which are presented in Table 2. The districts then obtain supplementary funding of 37,700 CAD per pupil in Level 1, of 18,850 CAD per pupil in Level 2 and of 9,500 CAD per pupil in Level 3. Details are provided in the chapter on support for special needs students below.

Supplement for other unique students' needs

Furthermore, there is a supplement for other unique students' needs. Students with such needs may be eligible to receive funding for Aboriginal Education (additional funding of 1,195 CAD per pupil) or English/French as a Second Language (1,380 CAD per pupil) if the requirements of these programs are met (Guiltner et al., 2008).

The province also provides supplements to fund services for "vulnerable students". These are determined from the following factors:
- economic conditions (65 percent weight in the calculation),
- demographic vulnerability (12.5 percent),
- social conditions (12.5 percent),
- and educational attainment (10 percent).

The economic conditions are measured by the share of people receiving income assistance (40 percent), being in deep poverty (30 percent), and being in moderate poverty (30 percent). The demographic vulnerability includes factors such as the share of the aboriginal population (50 percent), single parents (30 percent) or recent immigrants (20 percent). The social conditions include having children in care (60 percent), serious crimes (20 percent), suicide/homicide (20 percent). And lastly educational attainment is measured as the share of adults who have not graduated from high school. All these factors are taken into account and then, based on available resources, the province provides additional funding proportionally based on vulnerable student population sizes. In 2017/18, 25 out of 60 school districts received a total funding of 11.219 million CAD.[15]

Unique District

A supplement for a unique district consists of a small community supplement, a low enrolment factor, a rural factor, a climate factor, a sparseness factor, a student location factor, a supplemental student location factor and a salary differential.

---

15   See https://www2.gov.bc.ca/assets/gov/education/administration/community-partnerships/communitylink/communitylink_vss_funding.pdf.

Small community supplement
The small community supplement is provided in order to support primary schools in small districts. The rationale behind it is that smaller classes and smaller schools are costlier per student.[16] For regular[17] primary schools, the supplement is provided in cases when the full-time student equivalent population in a defined area – which is either a single school or all schools located within 5 kilometers by the shortest road – is less than 250 students. The population of students is measured as the previous year's enrolment. Specifically, a district receives:
- for each community with 8 or fewer primary full-time equivalent students: 78,250 CAD,
- for each community with 9 to 110 primary full-time equivalent students: 164,360 CAD,
- for each community with 110 to 250 primary full-time equivalent students: $164{,}360 - (1{,}160 \times (\text{the number of time equivalents students} - 110))$ CAD.

Furthermore, a district is eligible for funding for small remote schools if there is a community with 75 or fewer primary school-age full-time equivalent students and one of the following is fulfilled:
- the school is at least 40 kilometers by road from the next nearest primary school,
- the school is at least 5 kilometers from the next nearest primary school but accessible only by gravel road, logging road or by water;

Then a district receives 166,800 CAD for each community with 15 or fewer primary full-time equivalent students and 187,600 CAD for each community with 16 to 75 primary full-time equivalent students.

Low enrolment factor
The low enrolment factor is also determined using the enrolment numbers for the previous school year. A district with 2,500 or fewer school-age full-time equivalents receives 1,385,000 CAD and a district with more than 2,500, but fewer than 15,000 school-age full-time equivalents receives:
$$1{,}385{,}000 - (110.80 \times (\text{the number of full-time equivalent students} - 2{,}500))$$
$$\text{CAD}$$

Larger districts with more than 15,000 full-time equivalent students are not eligible.

---
16 In economics, the differences in costs per student would be explained as economies of scale.
17 Other types of schools are not eligible.

Rural factor

The rural factor supplement is only for districts that have a district education office at least 100 kilometers away from Vancouver by road. It is calculated (in %) as follows:

$$(5 - Population\ Scale) \times 100 + km\ to\ Vancouver + km\ to\ Regional\ Center \times previous\ year's\ Basic\ Allocation \times 0.2$$

So the factor is determined by the population of the city in which the district education office is located and the distances to Vancouver[18] and the nearest city with a minimum population of 70,000.

The index is then multiplied by the Basic Allocation from the previous year's funding for each school district, and finally the factor is weighted by 20 %.

Climate factor

The climate factor is calculated as follows:

$$(Total\ Climate\ Days - provincial\ minimum) \times previous\ year's\ Basic\ Allocation \times 0.05$$

Total Climate Days is given as the sum of the number of very cold (so-called Days of Cooling) and very warm days (so-called Days of Heating) between 1981 and 2010 for each district.[19] The provincial minimum is 2,748.3 Climate Days.

The index is then multiplied by the Basic Allocation from the previous year's funding for each school district, and finally the factor is weighted by 5 %.

Sparseness factor

The sparseness factor aims to address the additional costs arising from increased travel in districts where schools are separated from the district education office. The details of the calculation are provided in the Operating Grants Manual.[20]

The index is then again multiplied by the Basic Allocation from the previous year's funding for each school district, and finally the factor is weighted by 12 %.

---

18   Different weighting might be applied to the distances if there is water separation.
19   Detailed definitions of Total Climate Days etc. are provided in the Operating Grants Manual https://www2.gov.bc.ca/assets/gov/education/administration/resource-management/k12funding/17-18/17-18-operating-grants-manual.pdf.
20   https://www2.gov.bc.ca/assets/gov/education/administration/resource-management/k12funding/17-18/17-18-operating-grants-manual.pdf, p. 12.

Student location factor

The student location factor is additional funding that reflects the school-age population density of communities within a given district. The density weighted full-time equivalent students are calculated first.[21] A district receives:

$$258.75 \times weighted\ primary\ full\ time\ equivalent\ student\ \text{CAD}.$$

Districts with fewer than 500 weighted full-time equivalents (during the previous school year) receive a basic amount of 50,000 CAD.

Supplemental student location factor

This supplement is paid as an addition to the student location factor and is calculated as

$$5{,}000 \times nr.\ of\ Level\ 1\ special\ needs\ student + 1{,}000 \times nr.\ of\ Level\ 2\ special\ needs\ student,$$

the numbers of students are based on the previous school year's enrolments.

Supplement for salary differential

This supplement aims to address the differences in salaries across districts (a supplement is paid to districts with a higher average, no punishment to districts with a lower average) with higher average teacher salaries. The calculation of the supplement is simple:

$$Estimated\ number\ of\ educators\ in\ the\ district \times District\ salary\ differential$$

The estimated number of educators is calculated as the total district enrolment divided by the assumed average student/teacher ratio (18). District salary differential is calculated as the difference between the provincial average and the district's average salary.

Funding Protection / Enrolment Decline

This funding for enrolment decline is an additional amount for school districts with a funding decline larger than 1.5% (in comparison with the previous year funding).

If the total operating grants from the previous school year to the total operating grants for the current year decline by more than 1.5%, an additional funding protection is in place so that the year-to-year decline is no greater than 1.5%.

---

21 Details of the calculation are explained in the Operating Grants Manual https://www2.gov.bc.ca/assets/gov/education/administration/resource-management/k12funding/17-18/17-18-operating-grants-manual.pdf, p. 13.

Community LINK
CommunityLINK (Learning Includes Nutrition and Knowledge) is funding outside the Operating Grants (described above) that is meant to further support vulnerable students. It is proportionally (with respect to the number of vulnerable students) distributed to all districts. In 2017/18, the province distributed approximately 52 million CAD.

The funding is spent predominantly on services such as breakfasts, lunches and snack programs, academic support, counseling, youth workers and after-school programs.

Total per student funding
After accounting for all these factors, the funding formula generates very different per student funding for different districts. For example, while the funding per student in the district of Vancouver is around 8,000 CAD, the remote islands of Haida Gwaii receive almost 17,000 CAD per student, to recognize the various challenges they face there. In the following paragraph, we will discuss the district municipality of Mission. The population is about 38,833 and the area is 227.65 km² which makes the district similar to many small to middle-sized districts in Europe. The district includes many rural remote localities such as Silverdale, Silverhill or Ruskin.

An example a primary school budget in the district of Mission

In the following paragraph, we present an example of funding of the Deroche Elementary School. The funding presented below is based on real figures which were provided during the interviews.

In the 2016-2017 school year, there were 77 students enrolled in the school. In general, the district assumes a maximum of 24 students per class. However, in smaller schools, this might be impossible since there can be fewer students in a grade; therefore, the districts fund 4.9 full teachers' positions (assuming approximately a ratio of 15 students per teacher).

Besides funding for teachers, there is funding for supplies and services and for staff development. The funding for supplies and services includes basic elementary funding per school, funding for the library, art and physical education, textbooks, paper, supplies, photocopying and other allocations (learning resources and library). The staff development is funding used mostly for in-service training.

The funding for supplies and services consists of:

1. *Basic elementary funding per school* – this is given by the number of students. Schools with fewer than 200 full-time equivalent students (such as the Deroche school being studied) receive 1,840 CAD. Schools with more than 200 but fewer than 300 receive 1,710 CAD, schools with more than 300 but fewer than 400 receive 1,580 CAD, schools with more than 400 but fewer than 500 receive 1,450 CAD.
2. *Funding for library* – for schools with fewer than 300 students, the funding is 15 CAD per student and 10 CAD per student for larger schools. In the case of the Deroche school, this means 77×15 = 1,155 rounded up to 1,200 CAD.
3. *Funding for art and physical education* – for schools with fewer than 300 pupils, the funding is 8 CAD per student and 6 CAD per student for larger schools. In the case of the Deroche school, this implies 77×8 = 616 rounded down to 600 CAD.
4. *Funding for textbooks* – for schools with fewer than 300 students, the funding is 12 CAD per student and 10 CAD per student for larger schools. In the case of the Deroche school, this means 77×12 = 924 rounded down to 900 CAD.
5. *Funding for paper* - This is again given by the number of students. It is 1,500 CAD for schools with fewer than 100 students, 2,500 CAD for schools with 101 to 300 students and 3,500 for schools with over 300 students. So, it amounts to 1,500 CAD for the studied Deroche school.
6. *Funding for supplies* – This input is determined by the number of full-time equivalent students which is then multiplied by 5 CAD. In the case of the Deroche school, this means 77×5 = 385 rounded up to 400 CAD.
7. *Funding for photocopying* - It is given by the number of students. It equals 1,500 CAD for schools with fewer than 100 students, 5,250 CAD for school with 101 to 300 students and 8,250 for schools with over 300 students. So, it amounts to 1,500 CAD for the Deroche school.
8. *Other allocations for learning resources and library* - They are determined case by case, and were 5,000 CAD and 2,000 CAD for the Deroche school, respectively.

The staff development is determined as the number of full-time equivalent teachers × 200 augmented with a number of full-time equivalent enrolled students × 7. So in the case of the Deroche school, it amounts to 4.9 × 200 + 77 × 7 = 1,519. Both were rounded down to first hundreds so the final amount was 1,500 CAD.

FUNDING FORMULAS

The school, thus, in total receives funding for 4.9 full-time equivalent teachers, 14,940 CAD for supplies and services and 1,500 CAD for staff professional development.

Area	Calculation	Total funding (in CAD)
Basic elementary funding per school		1,840
Funding for library	77 (FTE students) × 15= 1,155	1,200
Funding for art and physical education	77 × 8 = 616	600
Funding for textbooks	77 × 12 = 924	900
Funding for paper		1,500
Funding for supplies	77 × 5 = 385	400
Funding for photocopying		1,500
Other allocations	5,000 + 2,000	7,000
Total		14,940

Table 3: Calculation of funding of Deroche Elementary School; source: Authors' representation of the data provided by Superintendent in the district of Mission.

Special needs students do not directly generate additional funding for the school. Most of the additional funding that is received by the district from the province of British Columbia is spent directly on educational assistants or medical/psychological testing, administration or physical devices. This is paid for by the district, not the school (under the direction of the Director of Student Services). So if we assume for instance one deaf-blind student – i.e. a student with special needs of level 1 – in Deroche Elementary School, the district would get additional funding of 37,700 CAD for this student and would use it directly for the needs of this student.

Secondary schools

The calculation of funding for secondary schools differs mostly in the calculation of the number of students for "Basic Allocation" and some aspects of the calculation of "Unique Student" and "Unique District" allocations. We focus on the description of the aspects of the calculation that are different, for the aspects that are identical we refer the reader to the previous sub-chapter.

Basic Allocation

As for primary schools, the Basic Allocation for secondary schools is a standard amount of money determined by the number of courses secondary school students are enrolled in in a school district, and it includes resources to support the needs of pupils who are identified *"as having learning disabilities, mild intellectual disabilities, students requiring moderate behaviour supports and students who are gifted"* (BC Ministry of Education, p.138, 2016).

The Basic Allocation per course is set to 1/8 of the Basic Allocation per eligible secondary school-age full-time equivalent (FTE) pupil. In the 2016/17 academic year, the per course allocation was 902.25[22] CAD (British Columbia, Resource Management Division, 2016). All courses are funded by the same amount.[23]

A regular full-time student takes 8 courses. However, it is possible that some students take only 7 courses, in which case a district is funded as to 7/8 of the full-time amount (in comparison with a full-time primary student or a secondary student who takes 8 courses). In other words, 100 secondary school students in a hypothetical district might – in terms of funding – be an equivalent of only 96.65 full-time primary school students. This number of full-time equivalent secondary students is then used in determining other funding such as unique district funding and so on.

There are very few compulsory courses such as math, language, arts and similar. No additional funds are specifically provided for vocational or technical courses, although some schools apply for special grants that work outside the standard funding formula.

Unique Student

In the same way as primary school students, some secondary school pupils with special needs may require additional support and funds on top of the Basic Allocation. There are the same 3 levels of special needs support (see Table 2). The calculation is identical to the one for a primary school.

Supplement for other unique students' needs

While the calculation of the supplement for other unique students' needs is identical to the calculation of the supplement for primary schools, the allocations for students with limited and/or no English (or French) are targeted to recent migrants and are funded for up to 5 years. This is not the case for primary school students.

---

22 = 7,218/8.
23 Note, however, that the costs of the courses vary widely, whether because of class size limits (for a science lab the limit is 24 students and for a math class the limit is 30) or, for instance, consumables.

The supplements to fund services for "vulnerable students" are calculated in the same way as for primary schools.

Unique District

A supplement for a unique district consists of a small community supplement, a low enrolment factor, a rural factor, a climate factor, a sparseness factor, a student location factor, a supplemental student location factor and salary differential. The difference compared to primary schools' funding is predominantly in the calculation of full-time equivalent students which is based on the number of courses the students are enrolled in (the calculation is done as described in the subchapter about Basic Allocation). Moreover, the exact amounts and coefficients for the small community supplement and student location factor differ; thereby, we focus on these three elements of the "Unique District" funding calculation. The other elements – i.e. low enrollment factor, rural factor, climate factor, sparseness factor, supplemental student location factor and supplement for salary differential – are identical to those for primary education.

Small community supplement

The small community supplement for secondary schools serves the same function as for primary schools, i.e. it is provided to schools in small districts as smaller classes and schools are supposed to be costlier per students. For regular secondary schools, the supplement is provided in cases when a full-time student equivalent population in a defined area – which is either a single school or all schools located within 25 kilometers by the shortest road distance – is less than 635 students. The population of students is measured on the previous year's enrolment. Specifically, a district receives:
- for each community with 100 or fewer secondary full-time equivalent students:

    $4,681.25 \times$ *the number of time equivalent students* CAD

- for each community with 100 to 635 secondary full-time equivalent students:

    $468,125 - (875 \times$ *(the number of time equivalent students – 100))* CAD.

Furthermore, a district is eligible for funding for grades 11 and 12 small community funding. A community eligible for the small community supplement as described above with students in grades 11 and/or 12 receives:
- for each community with 15 or fewer secondary full-time equivalent students in grades 11 and/or 12:

    $12,600 \times$ *the number of time equivalent students* CAD

- for each community with 15 to 215 secondary full-time equivalent students:
$189,000 - (945 \times (\text{the number of time equivalent students} - 15))$ CAD.

Student location factor
The student location factor is meant to reflect the secondary school-age population density of communities within a given district. The density weighted full-time equivalent students are calculated at first.[24] A district receives:
$340.67 \times \text{weighted secondary full-time equivalent student}$ CAD.

Districts with fewer than 500 weighted full-time equivalent students (during the previous school year) receive a base amount of 50,000 CAD.

Funding Protection / Enrolment Decline
This funding for enrolment decline is calculated in the same way as for primary schools.

In-service training
The district also manages educational funds that are used for in-service training. Schools get a small amount of funds (currently the amount is set at 210 CAD per teacher and 10 CAD per student) for individual professional development of teachers, and a larger pool for professional development determined by the teachers' union in consultation with the district. District initiatives are determined by senior staff in consultation with principals and teachers. In addition, the district gives 155 CAD per full-time equivalent teacher to the Mission Teachers' Union each year, and these funds are then managed by the teachers' union. The district also organizes itself in-service training when it provides resources, teaching materials etc. These funds are directly controlled by the district.

> **An example of a secondary school budget in the district of Mission**
>
> In the following paragraph, we present an example of funding of the Mission secondary school. The funding presented below is based on real figures which were provided during the interviews.

---

24 Details of the calculation are explained in the Operating Grants Manual https://www2.gov.bc.ca/assets/gov/education/administration/resource-management/k12funding/17-18/17-18-operating-grants-manual.pdf, p. 13.

> In the 2016-2017 school year, there were 1,434.25 full-time equivalent students enrolled in the school. In order to keep the ratio of approximately 21 students to 1 teacher, the districts funds 66.6849 full-time teachers' positions.
>
> Besides funding for teachers, there is basic secondary funding for supplies and services and funding for staff development. The staff development is funding used mostly for in-service training.
>
> The funding for supplies and services consists of:
> 1. *Basic secondary funding per school* – this is given by rounding up the number of students to hundreds of CAD. The school receives 190 CAD per student, i.e. 1,434.25 × 190 = 272,500 CAD.
> 2. *Other allocations for learning resources, library and international cooperation* – These were set to 15,000 CAD, 6,000 CAD and 20,000 CAD, respectively.
>
> The staff development is determined as the number of full-time equivalent teachers × 210 augmented by a number of full-time equivalent enrolled students × 10. So in the case of the Mission Secondary, it amounts to 66.6849 × 210 + 1,434.25 × 10. Both were rounded down to first hundreds so the final amount was 28,300 CAD.
>
> The school, thus, in total receives funding for 66.6849 full-time equivalent teachers, 313,500 CAD for supplies and services and 28,300 CAD for staff professional development.

Support for special needs students

The legal basis for additional funding for students with special needs is the School Act Section 106.3 (5) and the Ministerial Order M150/89 ("the Special Needs Students Order"). The necessary level of support for pupils with special needs may vary. In order to account for this variation in needs, 3 different levels were established. The levels and the associated disabilities are shown in Table 2.

School districts report pupils with special needs. Such pupils must be assessed, identified as coming within one of these 3 levels and have an Individual Education Plan (IEP). The additional funding is received by the districts. The amount of additional resources differs for different levels and is obtained on per pupil basis.

The districts in British Columbia obtain supplementary funding of 37,700 CAD per pupil in Level 1, of 18,850 CAD per pupil in Level 2 and of 9,500 CAD per pupil in Level 3. These amounts do not differ for primary and secondary school pupils.

A case study on special needs funding in the district of Mission

In the following paragraph, we present an example of funding of the Deroche Elementary School with the focus on special needs students. We will not review the funding not related to special needs.

Special needs students do not directly generate additional funding for the school. Most of the additional funding that is received by the district from the province of British Columbia is spent directly on educational assistants or medical/psychological testing, administration or physical devices. This is paid by the district, not the school (under the direction of the Director of Student Services). So if we assume for instance one deaf-blind student – i.e. a student with special needs of level 1 – in Deroche Elementary School, the district would get additional funding of 37,700 CAD for that student and would use it directly for the needs of that student.

A case-study of the funding formula in the district of Mission[25]

As mentioned already earlier, the funds are transferred to districts, not directly to schools. Thus, we provide a case study of how the funding of schools works in the district of Mission.

Primary schools
The main aim of funding in the district of Mission, just like provincial funding, is to support equality of opportunity for all learners. The districts provide basic staffing to primary schools primarily based on enrolment from a ratio of an average of 27 students to 1 teacher. Thus, for instance, a primary school with 300 students would receive funding for 11 teachers on staff. The district also sets class size limits that vary by grade level and subject. In primary education from grades 1 to 3, the limit is 24 students in class at the maximum and from grades 4 to 7, it is 30 students. The maximum class size is reduced by 1 for having a student with special needs in the class. The maximum reduction of the class size is by 3; however, if a class has more than 3 students with special needs other specific allowances are put in place.

Based on a Collective Agreement, the district is required to staff certain amounts of time for Teacher-Librarians, Music, and Special Education.

---

25   This detailed information about the funding formula in Mission was provided by Angus Wilson, Superintendent in the district of Mission in British Columbia.

A school, further, receives administrative time for the School Principal (reserved for responsibilities other than teaching) based on the number of students, but on a declining rate. At 275 students, a school gets 1.0 FTE administrative time and the school is triggered into getting a Vice Principal at 300 students. As the number of students moves from 50 students towards 275, how much of 1.0 FTE the school gets is increased. For instance, at 100 students a school gets approximately 0.6 FTE and at 200 it gets 0.9.

School-based budgets for site-based purchases are generated by the enrolment. Secondary schools get in general more than elementary schools. The money is calculated by the number of full-time equivalent students and typically runs from 25,000 CAD up to 1,000,000 CAD depending on school size.

Furthermore, schools in the district of Mission can ask for capital funds (such as for maintenance, planning and similar). This spending is centrally controlled by the district. It reviews the needs of the schools and attempts to allocate funds based on need.

In-service training
The district also manages educational funds that are used for in-service training. Schools get a small amount of funds (currently the amount is set to 200 CAD per teacher) for the individual professional development of teachers, and a larger pool for professional development determined by the teachers' union in consultation with the district. District initiatives are determined by senior staff in consultation with principals and teachers. In addition, the district gives 155 CAD per full-time equivalent teacher to the Mission Teachers' Union every year and these funds are then managed by the teachers' union.

The district also organizes in-service training itself when it provides resources, teaching materials etc. These funds are directly controlled by the district.

Supplements for transport, school trips and sports
Mission runs school buses for rural students to get to school. A fee is charged – from 200 to 400 CAD per year. The fee is waived if the family demonstrates economic need (this is families making less thana certain amount, 24,000 to 39,000 CAD depending on family size).

The funds for school trips and sports are controlled by schools. However, the district keeps small additional funds to ensure that activities that have costs associated with them (for example, a trip to the museum or a soccer game in Vancouver) are compensated for so that students in poverty do not need to pay.

Other special programs
The district further receives specific targeted funds for certain programming, such as "StrongStart", an early childhood education program. These are effectively money in, money out – i.e. the money from the provincial government is 100 percent spent on this specific program. Local control is only in determining how many "StrongStart" Mission can have, and placing them in the various buildings.

The determination of the next year's budget for schools in the Mission district
Every year between March and May, the Committee of the Whole, comprised of the Board of Education, senior district staff, and representatives from unions, principals, educational partners, and the community at large, meet every other week to discuss the next year's budget.

Additional funds for a special project, a particular educational initiative, technology refresh, and the like all go through the process of evaluation by the Committee. Such process is transparent since it is decided when all interest groups are present. On the other hand, such process to determine the budget is time-consuming.

Secondary schools
The funding formula provides basic staffing for secondary schools based on enrolment from a ratio of an average of 21 students to 1 teacher. In particular, there are approximately 67 full-time teachers for about 1,434 students.

As for primary schools, the budget for site-based purchases is also generated by the enrolment and managed by the district. Secondary schools receive, in general, more than primary schools.

Capital spending is – as in the case of primary schools – centrally controlled by the district. It reviews the needs of the schools and attempts to allocate such spending based on need.

Typically secondary schools require greater funding not just because of their size, but due to their programming—things like metalwork, science labs, etc. Further, a school in a more challenging neighborhood can receive funding for additional counsellors, after-school programs, etc. In general, the enrolment determines approximately 90 or more percent of the school's funding.

In-service training
The amounts paid to secondary schools for in-service training are also slightly higher. In particular, in 2017 the amount was set at 210 CAD per teacher and

10 CAD per student. The funding is intended for the individual professional development of teachers. District initiatives are determined by senior staff in consultation with principals and teachers. In addition, also for secondary school teachers the district gives 155 CAD per full-time equivalent teacher to the Mission Teachers' Union every year.

Special needs students and other additional student-focused funding
Even though it is the districts that receive the unique students' funding, the funding is generated and directed per individual student. That is, a parent in Mission should be able to be shown how this additional funding (9,500 to 37,700 CAD according to the level of the student's special needs) his/her child generates is allocated to the child. Most of this funding is spent on educational assistants or medical/psychological testing, administration or physical devices. It is spent by the district under the direction of the Director of Student Services.[26] She ensures that the student in question is getting adequate support. As a general rule, the more spread out and rural a district is, the more decentralized this spending becomes.

The aforementioned supplement for other unique students includes Aboriginal Education. These funds are also spent centrally by the district by the Principal of Aboriginal Education.

All schools are, further, allocated "First Nations Resource Workers". A share of the core funding (the amount that is determined by the number of full-time equivalent students) is also partly used to pay the Principal's salary and Halq'emeylem teachers (the language of the local First Nation, the Sto:lo people). However, schools receive additional funds to support the language. Specifically, every student that identifies as First Nations/Inuit/Metis generates an additional 1,100 CAD per year. This money is spent on things like First Nations Resource Workers, Language Support workers, Consumables, Indigenous Cultural support and so on. About 20 percent of students in the district have indigenous ancestry, but some schools have significantly larger populations or ratios, and thus are allocated greater resources.

Additional staffing and resources are allocated by the Superintendent of the district of Mission by determining the Social Services Index of the school. This is a measure of the "at risk" function of students. Thus, an 'inner city' school with a vulnerable population will be given "bonus" staffing in the form of more Principal administration time, lower student-teacher ratios,

---

26 So it is not the schools that receive or manage this money.

district support, and so on, in comparison to a more economically advantaged community neighborhood.

Summary of the education funding system in British Columbia and the district of Mission

In British Columbia, the basic allocation is predominantly determined by the number of primary school age pupils enrolled in a school district and by the number of courses provided by secondary school districts. It also includes funding for most students with special needs including gifted students. Given the large variety in the size of districts and population density, the province faces a big challenge in distributing appropriate funds to the districts. Therefore, it takes into account various unique geographic factors and provides supplements for schools in small communities. These are provided based on geographical distances from other schools, not just by the size of a school (which is different from the practice in Estonia, see Chapter 4.2) and it makes the funding formula less prone to support small schools that could easily merge.

Below, we summarize some strengths and weaknesses of the funding formula in British Columbia. Furthermore, Figure 2 shows the main determinants of the total allocation from the province to a school district.

STRENGTHS	WEAKNESSES
1. The system rather discourages over-identification of special needs students as most of them are included in the basic allocation; 2. The system in general reflects very well the geographical and other differences between districts.	1. Allowances for declining enrollment are sometimes too generous, allowing districts to 'coast' rather than implement changes due to the reality of smaller student numbers; 2. The funding formula does not really reward innovation or marked improvements; thus it is supporting the status quo.

On the district level, funding is to a large part determined based on class size and funding for teaching staff that is necessary to keep this number of classes. The district, furthermore, also funds a certain number of Teacher-Librarians, Music teachers, and, importantly, it directly hires educational assistants for special needs students. A parent of such a student in Mission should be able to be shown how the funds are allocated to the child and how they are spent.

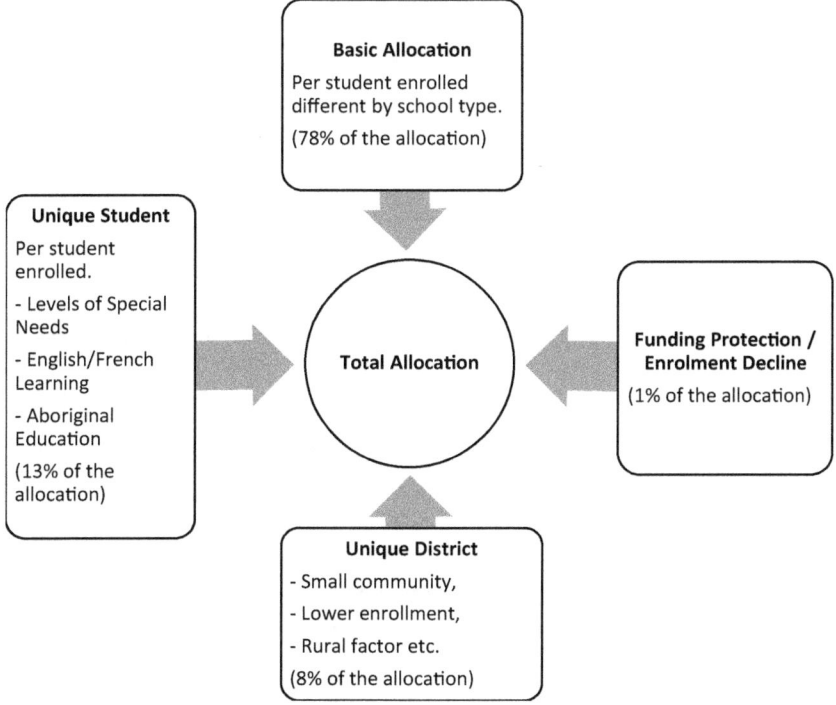

Figure 2: Simplified diagram of the main determinants of total allocation to school districts in British Columbia; source: Authors.

4.2 Estonia

Estonia has been gradually coming to per capita funding of general education during 1990s with two reforms in 1994 and 1998. The school population as well as the number of students attending the Estonian general and vocational secondary schools continued to decrease (see Figure 3), as did class and school sizes. Thus, reforms to keep sufficient funding for such schools were introduced. The 2008 Estonian funding formula essentially removed the per capita element for small rural schools and used a per class basis system, which makes this formula an interesting case-study of how the political preference for keeping small rural schools might hamper the efficiency incentives of a funding formula (Levačić, 2011). Thus, first we will introduce the 2008 formula with the focus on the per class basis of the funding (note that in this part vocational schools, that as general secondary schools educate students in grades 10 to 12, are not considered) before the current funding formula

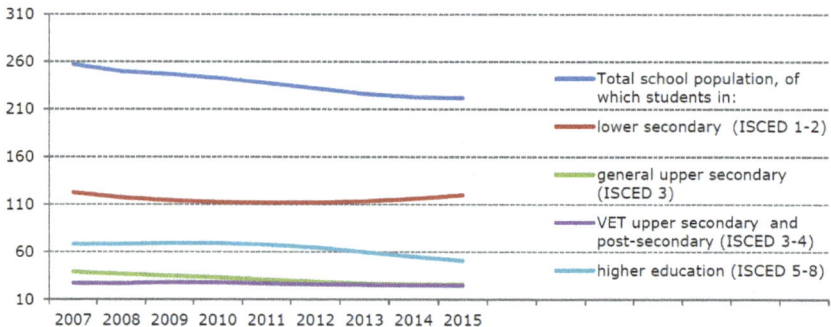

Figure 3: Secondary school population (the number of students in thousands is on the vertical axis) in Estonia; source: European Commission (2016).

(starting in 2012) – which mostly returned to the per student system with fixed coefficients – is discussed. In this final part, we also include information about vocational education.

The current formula does not have clear separate components like the one in, for instance, British Columbia (Basic Allocation, Unique Student etc.). However, it assumes 20 percent extra resources, 21 lessons per teacher on average and 24 students in class on average. These basic assumptions yield per student allocations that are weighted by fixed coefficients calculated in 2012 using the old formula that was class-based especially for small rural schools.

Primary schools

The 2008 Estonian funding formula

The revised version of the 2008 Estonian funding formula was in force until 2012. The major revision of the previous funding formula was done mainly because some (small) municipalities were criticizing the fact that the formula did not take into account the expenditure needs of municipalities with small schools or schools with small classes. The previous formula was based mainly on the size of municipalities. It did not take into account the distribution of pupils between grades within the schools and assumed the same expenditure for pupils of all ages, which is not reasonable at least because of the higher number of classes per week for older students (Levačić, 2011).

The 2008 formula was favorable to municipalsities with fewer than 1,600 students in one of the main languages of instruction — Estonian and Russian. The municipalities in this category were funded according to the number of classes that were needed to be organized according to the formula, given the number of pupils in each grade. The larger municipalities – i.e. those having more than 1,600 pupils – were funded per student. The formula treated Estonian and Russian pupils separately provided that they were taught in separate classes.[27] The number and size of the classes were not set by the formula or the law; however, funding remained based on the assumed number of classes. The actual number of classes created by the schools was not taken into account for funding. So, municipalities could sustain smaller primary schools and classes provided that they chose to allocate funds to support the additional teaching costs.

The calculation of the funding in the 2008 Estonian funding formula
The education grant according to the 2008 formula can be split into two parts in order to work out the allocated amount per student. First, it is an allocation for the basic minimum amount that covers teaching and the other resources that a school must provide according to the law (this includes textbooks, workbooks, investments etc.). And, second, it is an additional amount that is for local governments to use according to their own policy choices in education. This is about 10 percent of the total allocation and it is derived from the left-over amount after subtracting the first part from the total allocated amount. So, this additional funding is only artificially separated for the purposes of explaining the formula. In reality, it is included in the per student calculated amount (Levačić, 2011).

Funding per student differs for 3 stages (according to the grades) in primary education as they were introduced in the overview of education systems. In Table 4, we present the per student funding amount calculation. Column 1 gives the number of compulsory lessons taught per week to classes in respective grades (e.g. in grades from 1 to 3, the pupils must be taught 68 lessons per week). In Column 2, there is the number of teachers assuming that a teacher teaches on average 21 lessons per week. This number is then multiplied by the cost of a teacher in order to get the total costs of teachers which is in Column 3. The teachers' cost is assumed to be the basic salary of a regular teacher including unemployment insurance (we use the figure from 2008), other labor taxes paid by employers and in-service training (36.3 percent). Finally, in order to obtain the per student amount, the number from Column 3 is divided by the class sizes in the respective grades. The minimum size of a class is 17 students in primary schools and the formula generates enough resources for a school with this class size. Column 4 then shows the average per student allocation for the different grades based on the total cost of teachers calculation.

---

27 We use the exchange rate EEK/EUR = 0.06387082763, as of September 1, 2008. Retrieved from http://statistika.eestipank.ee/?lng=en#treeMenu/VALUUTA.

Grades/ Stages	Compulsory lessons per week	Teachers needed	Total costs of teachers	Per student amount [EEK]	Total per student amount [EEK]
1-3	68	3.2	533,505	10,461	11,455 (731.64 EUR[28])
4-5	83	4.0	651,190	12,768	13,982 (893.04 EUR)
6-9	93	4.6	753,183	14,768	16,172 (1,032.92 EUR)

Table 4: Calculation of per student funding; source: Levačić (2011).

The figures calculated in Column 4 of Table 4, were then enhanced by the second part – the additional funding. This amount changes over time depending on the available funds, and in 2008 it was 9.5 percent. The total per student amounts for basic teaching are in Column 5.

Additional funding for municipalities smaller than 1600 students
Municipalities that have fewer than 1,600 students attending Estonian- or Russian-speaking schools receive funds based on the assumed number of small classes as long as the grade has 33 or fewer students. For grades 1-9, a small class is 17 students. Such municipalities with small classes receive additional funding for "empty places" in those small classes. This funding is provided only for primary education. Table 5 below provides an overview of the additional funding for small classes.

Number of students per grade	1-16	17	18-23	24-26	27-33	34-35	36-47
Number of assumed classes formed	1 small	1 small	1 full	1 full	2 small	2 small	2 full
Funding	P + A	P	P + A	P	P + A	P	P

Table 5: Additional funding for small classes; Note: P = per student funding; A = additional funding; source: Levačić (2011).

Additional funding for small classes
Furthermore, in grades 1-5, it is assumed that in schools with grades with fewer than 7 pupils, students of 2 or 3 grades will be combined in one class. However, if this is not sufficient to create a class of 17 students, the school would receive additional funding based on empty places, but the maximum that can be provided is three times the per student funding. So,

---

28 We use the exchange rate EEK/EUR = 0.06387082763, as of September 1, 2008. Retrieved from http://statistika.eestipank.ee/?lng=en#treeMenu/VALUUTA.

for instance, a school with a grade with only 1 student can get a maximum of 3 times per student allocation (i.e. the additional funding is provided for 2 empty spaces in a class – in total 3 times per student allocation, not 16 empty spaces up to the minimum class size of 17 students). Thus, in the end, the cut of the additional funding is applied only for classes smaller than or equal to 5 students (since by having 6 students per 3 grades means that a school can combine classes that reach the minimum of 17 that is then fully funded). Following the example from Levačić (2011), a primary school having just one student in each of grades 1 to 6 can combine them into one class since it gets 6 times 3 the per student funding. This applies only for grades 1 to 6; there is no additional funding for higher grades with fewer than 10 students.

Allocation for school directors and deputies

The number of funded school directors and deputy posts can be determined from Table 6.

Number of students	Number of classes	Posts
1-74	1	0.1
	2-3	0.25
	4	0.5
75-99		1
100-199		1.5
200-49		2
350-599		2.5
600 and more		3

Table 6: Funding for school directors and deputies; source: Levačić (2011).

A full-time director was funded at 1.4 times the teacher's basic salary, which was also the minimum salary for a director. As seen in Table 6, in small schools directors needed to teach since they were not funded highly enough to have full-time positions. However, it was common also in bigger schools for directors often to teach at least a few lessons per week.

Furthermore, form teachers who were in charge of a class were funded with a bonus of 10 percent of teacher's basic pay. The municipalities got additional form teachers' funding calculated from the assumed number of classes in schools.

Split size schools
Schools with single managements that were split over multiple sites might have received funding calculated as if the sites were separate schools if requested by the municipality. This additional funding was provided if the sites were at least 10 kilometers apart for funding for grades 1-5 and at least 30 kilometers for funding for grades 6-9.

Additional funding
Schools in sparsely populated and isolated areas might have received additional funding for regionally important schools which is meant to compensate teachers who could not have been given a full-time contract and they cannot obtain another part-time contract in a different school since it is too far away. These schools were funded additionally for small classes.

A similar system based on additional funding for small classes was used in order to determine the additional funding for special needs students, since the regulations required special needs students to be taught in smaller classes. The details about special needs education funding are provided in the sub-chapter below.

The current funding formula
The funding according to the current formula is as before received by municipalities from the central government and has four components: funding for salaries of teachers and school directors, funding for professional development of teachers and school directors, funding for school lunches, and funding for study materials (textbooks). The funding flow to primary and secondary schools is shown in Figure 4.

Education is currently mostly regulated by the Basic Schools and Upper Secondary Schools Act (2010, § 82 (3)) which states that *"the expenses of a municipal school are covered by the owner of the school. Based on the number of students of municipal schools, the support to be allocated to rural municipalities and cities for covering the labour expenses and in-service training expenses of the teachers, heads and head teachers of the municipal schools and the expenses relating to educational literature are determined annually in accordance with the State Budget Act."*

As explained above, the 2008 formula stressed the importance of keeping small schools in rural areas. This, however, might hamper the efficiency of the educational system. Therefore, in 2012, the Estonian government again changed the formula and returned to the per student funding-based formula. As before, the formula is designed to provide additional funding for smaller municipalities; however, the new formula incentivizes municipalities to consolidate their school networks (Santiago, 2016).

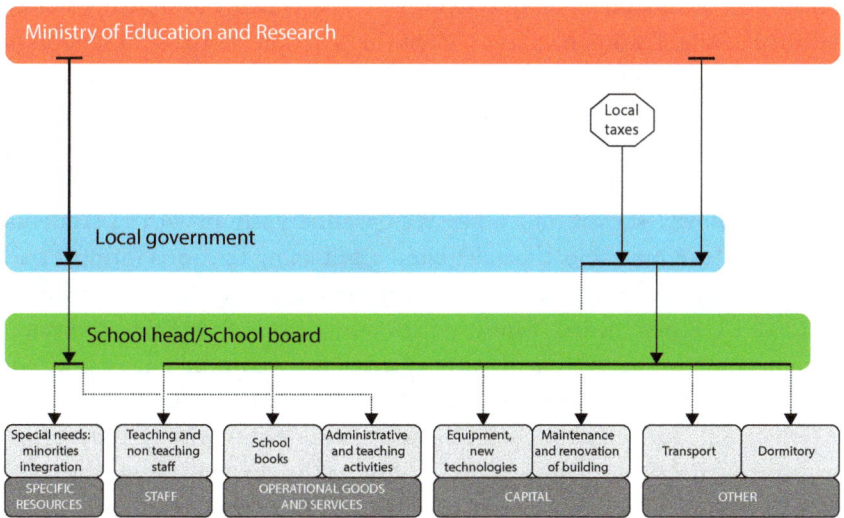

Figure 4: Flow of funding from Estonian municipalities to primary and secondary schools; source: European Commission/EACEA/Eurydice (2014).

The grant per student is the same for all municipalities except the grant for teachers' salary. For every municipality, there has been calculated a special coefficient to take into account their extra need per student because of the smaller classes. For primary education, coefficients vary between 1 and 2.05. These coefficients were calculated (using the 2008 formula from above) in 2014 and has been left the same afterwards.

Teachers' salary funding calculation

In order to compute the grant for teachers' salary, the funding formula (as in the 2008 formula) uses the number of full-time professional staff that is needed to teach the national curricula for different grades and levels of education. Class sizes are used to determine the number of teachers needed, which, in turn, translates to the funding for teaching positions which municipalities with given student populations receive.

For basic education, the teachers' salaries allocated according to the formula are calculated using an assumption that the average class should have "*24 students for municipalities with a student-teacher ratio equal or above 15; 21 students for municipalities with a student-teacher ratio between 7.8 and 14.9; and 10 students for municipalities with a student-teacher ratio of 7.7 or below*" (Santiago, 2016, p. 116). The assumed class sizes are, subsequently, adjusted by coefficients that reflect the need for additional teaching time (i.e. additional funding) for special needs students and students who take classes in Estonian (mostly ethnic Russian Estonian citizens whose instruction language in schools is Russian). This computation gives the number of teaching hours needed, which is then multiplied by the Estonian minimum teacher salary and multiplied by 1.2 to determine the teaching staff funding for a municipality (Santiago, 2016).

A simple illustration of the calculation of the coefficients for primary schools follows. The formula takes as a baseline a school with 24 students for all grades from 1 to 9, the calculated grant using the 2008 formula and the basic teachers' salary in 2014 would be 222,000 EUR which is equivalent to 1,028 EUR per student funding (222,000 / (9x24)). Making the same computation for a school with only 15 students, we would have a grant of 201,050 EUR which is equivalent to 1,489 EUR per student funding (201,050 / (9x15)). Subsequently, the coefficient for a municipality with 15 students per class is calculated as 1,489/1,028 = 1.45. And in the current system, the coefficients computed in this way have been frozen since 2014 despite subsequent changes in the number of students.

The calculation of transfers to school districts

The total amount is simply computed on a per student basis with coefficients used as weights:

number of students × coefficient × per student sum

The per student sum is given as

the average number of lessons needed per class per week × teacher's minimum salary × 1.2 × taxes × 12 / 21 / 24

where 1.2 stands for 20 percent extra resources, 12 for the number of months since the salary was given as monthly salary, 21 is the average number of lessons per teacher in a week and 24 the assumed number of students in a class. The special needs students cofficients are computed from the same formula; they simply assume a different class size.

An example of a primary school budget in Estonia

This box presents an example of a budget of an Estonian school. The basic calculation of funded lessons in grades 1-9 is described in Table 7. In this example, we assume a school with 180 students and that its students are spread equally across the grades, i.e. there are 20 students in each grade.

> The calculation of funding is based on the calculation of the need for lessons which then translates to the number of teachers and, consequently, the funding needed.
>
> In the example (see Table 7), the school needs 23.7×3, 36.0×3 and 41.0×3 lessons for all 9 grades. In order to calculate the necessary funding per student, we multiply the number of lessons × teacher's minimum salary × 1.2 × taxes × 12 / 21 / 24. As before, 1.2 stands for 20 percent extra resources, 12 for the number of months, 21 the average number of lessons per teacher in a week and 24 the assumed number of students in class.
>
> Assuming the teacher's minimum salary to be 958 EUR (as in 2016) and labor taxes of 36.3 percent, the school would receive 23.7 × 958 × 1.2 × 1.363 × 12 / 21 / 24 = 884 EUR for students in grades 1-3, 1,343 EUR for students in grades 4-6 and 1,530 EUR for students in grades 7-9. In total, this means that the school would receive 884×60 + 1,343×60 + 1,530×60 = 225,420 EUR.
>
> While other regions and countries (e.g., Flanders or some Nordic countries) take into account many additional criteria of students' backgrounds including the number of students from low income families, from single parent families, minority etc., this is not the case in Estonian municipalities.
>
> **Note:** If there are many schools in a district, it is considered necessary to keep the system competitive and effective. Then, a district component could be added. The main idea is that the calculations are based on the number of students in grades in a single educational district and their distribution between schools is not taken into account anymore. No school in the district is then funded per student more than the smallest funding calculated as in the case when all students were in one school. A single educational district consists of districts in which the closest schools (in the same study language) are less than x km apart or decided separately for different areas.

Secondary schools

The calculation of the funding in the 2008 Estonian funding formula
The calculation of funding for secondary schools follows the principles from primary education. It has also been reformed and the current version is presented in the subsection bellow. In Table 8, we present the per student funding for general secondary schools (grades 10-12).

Number of students in single grade at single educational district	Supported lessons			
	Stage I (Grades 1-3)	Stage II (Grades 4-6)	Stage I (Grades 7-9)	
1-10	2.27 lessons per student	2.77 lessons per student	3.13 lessons per student	The funding covers minimum costs if a school has 10 students per class. For example, a school with 5 students will get 5/10 of needed funding and, therefore, is forced to make mixed classes. Note: The number of lessons stated here is without the separate lessons.
11-19	22.7 + (number of students – 10) × 0.1	27.7 + (number of students – 10) × 0.83	31.3 + (number of students – 10) × 0.97	The number of supported lessons increases according to the number of students per grade.
20-24	23.7	36.0	41.0	The number of lessons for a full-size class that has separate lessons (language, gymnastics, manual training).
27-39	45.3 + (number of students / 2 – 10) × 0.2	55.3 + (number of students / 2 – 10) × 1.67	62.7 + (number of students / 2 – 10) × 1.93	2 small classes
40-48	47.3	72.0	82.0	2 full classes
53-59	68.6 + (number of students / 3 – 10) × 0.3	88 + (number of students / 3 – 10) × 2.5	99.8 + (number of students / 3 – 10) × 2.9	3 small classes
60-72	71.0	108.0	123.0	3 full classes
79-96	94.7	144.0	164.0	4 full classes
25-26; 49-52; 72-78; 97...	0.99 lessons per student	1.5 lessons per student	1.71 lessons per student	Oversized classes (normal maximum class size is 24 in Estonia) or 5+ classes per grade.

Table 7: Funding of schools with students in grades 1-9; source: own representation of the information provided by Andrus Jõgi, advisor at the Department of Financial Management of Local Governments of the Estonian Ministry of Finance.

Grades/ stages	Compulsory lessons per week	Teachers needed	Total costs of teachers	Per student amount [EEK]	Total per student amount [EEK]
10-12	105	5.0	823,794	13,076	14,319 (914.57 EUR[29])

Table 8: Calculation of per student funding; source: Levačić (2011).

Additional funding for municipalities smaller than 1,600 students that is provided for primary schools is not provided for secondary schools. Furthermore, secondary schools do not receive additional funding for split schools, as was the case for primary schools.

Allocation for school directors and deputies
The number of funded school directors and deputies' posts is determined identically as for primary school: see Table 6.

The current funding formula
The funding for secondary schools follows similar principles and laws as for primary education, so the grant per student is the same for all municipalities except the grant for teachers' salary. However, for upper secondary level, the coefficients are from 1 to 1.12 based on the total number of students in the municipality (compared to the coefficients varying between 1 and 2.05 for primary schools). These coefficients were calculated (using the 2008 formula from above) in 2014 and have been left the same since.

Teachers' salary funding calculation
The assumed class sizes are used to calculate the number of teachers and teaching hours, which are then multiplied by the Estonian minimum teacher's salary and multiplied by 1.2 to determine the teaching staff funding for a municipality (Santiago, 2016).

The total number of transfers for general secondary schools is calculated in the identical way as for primary schools.

Re-centralization of general secondary education
According to Santiago, P. et al. (2016), local governments have been slow to respond to the falling enrolment and consolidate secondary schools. The

---

29 We use the exchange rate EEK/EUR = 0.06387082763, as of September 1, 2008. Retrieved from http://statistika.eestipank.ee/?lng=en#treeMenu/VALUUTA.

Estonian government has recently decided to re-centralize general upper secondary education. And it established state-run *gymnasiums* in all county capitals. This is the opposite to the step that is planned for the primary schools where the government plans to give even more autonomy to the municipalities. Furthermore, it is also expected that the state will again also run special and vocational schools.

According to the new plan by 2020, the municipalities take full responsibility for pre-primary and primary education and the state for general and vocational secondary as well as special schools.

Vocational education and its funding
Vocational education is already mostly run by the Estonian state as it runs 30 out of 33 vocational education and training schools (Santiago, P. et al., 2016). The vocational schools run by local government are funded based on special coefficients that differ for the particular type of study. These coefficients (as in the formula for primary and general secondary education) were designed to align the funding with the number of teaching hours necessary for a given type of education, which makes the formula flexible to adjustments in curricula or per class norms.

Besides the state- and municipality-run schools, there are 5 private vocational schools. They typically provide education in highly subscribed areas such as information technologies, catering, or hairdressing (Santiago, P. et al., 2016).

For the 2016/17 school year, the base cost of a program per full-time student in vocational education was set at 1,665 EUR. The following mechanism is then used to calculate the total allocation:

number of students × coefficient × basic cost

The coefficients vary, ranging from 1.0 to 4.0 depending on curriculum group and study. For instance, for music and the performing arts the coefficient is set at 4.0; very high coefficients are also for media technologies and design (both 2.6). The lowest coefficient (1.0.) applies for trade and business services (see all coefficients at https://www.riigiteataja.ee/aktilisa/1210/2201/4020/VV_28m_lisa.pdf; in Estonian). The funding allocations calculated using this mechanism cover salaries, training materials and maintenance. The base costs are re-calculated every year. (Cedefop, 2017).

> **An example of a secondary school budget in Estonia**
>
> This box presents an example of a simplified budget of an Estonian vocational school (as for a general upper secondary school, the calculation would be very similar to that for a primary school, we rather present the vocational school budget calculation). In this example, we assume a school with 180 students of whom 60 study "Music and performing arts", 60 "Media technologies" and the remaining 60 "Design and crafts".
>
> The calculation is based on the coefficients for particular programs and the base cost set for the particular year. The coefficients are:
> - 4.0 for "Music and performing arts",
> - 2.6 for "Media technologies",
> - 2.6 for "Design and crafts".
>
> The basic funding determined by the number of students is thus as follows:
> - 60 students in "Music and performing arts" – 60 × 4.0 × 1,665 = 399,600 EUR.
> - 60 students in "Media technologies" – 60 × 2.6 × 1,665 = 259,740 EUR.
> - 60 students in "Design and crafts" – 60 × 4.0 × 1,665 = 259,740 EUR.
>
> Thus, the total funding for all 180 students is 919,080 EUR.

Special needs schools

Funding under the 2008 system
A similar system to that for additional funding for small classes for primary and general education was used to determine the additional funding for special needs students. The underlying reasoning is that special needs students need to be taught in smaller classes, which was also required by the regulations. The assumed maximum number of students in class depended on the type of special educational needs – specifically the limits were 7, 12 and 16.

Taking an example from Levačić (2011), we will now illustrate how the calculation worked. In a school with 14 special needs students for whom the maximum class size was 7, two classes were created and funded as two 17-student regular classes.

Funding of special schools
There are two types of special needs education for which the funding also works differently. These are state special needs schools and municipal special needs schools.

The state special needs schools receive funding based on a per student formula. This funding should fully cover the operating costs of the school.

The municipal special needs schools receive their funding based on the same principles as the mainstream schools (that are also funded via municipalities). So it has the same four components: funding for salaries of teachers and school directors, funding for professional development of teachers and school directors, funding for school lunches, and funding for study materials (textbooks). Operational costs are covered by municipalities.

In both cases of state and municipal special needs schools, the coefficients in the formula are designed to reflect the severity of the disability and the type of curriculum the student is being taught. The coefficients are summarized in Table 9.

Grade/type of education	Number of students in class	Coefficient
Basic education (grades 1-9)	12	1.79[30]
	8	2.43
	6	3.40
	4	3.58
	1	14.30
Upper secondary (9-12)	12	2.66

Table 9: Coefficients for special needs students; source: RiigiTeataja et al. (2017).

The calculation of transfer is then identical to the one for primary schools. Only the coefficients are different.

An example of a an additional funding calculation for special needs students in Estonia

This box presents an example of an additional funding calculation for special needs students in an Estonian school. We assume a primary school with 180 students and that its students are spread across the grades equally, i.e. there are 20 students in each grade. According to the calculations provided above (in a box for primary schools), the school would receive 884×60 + 1,343×60 + 1,530×60 = 225,420 EUR for all students without special needs.

If there was one special needs student that required one-to-one education in the school on top of the 180 students considered above, the school would

---

30 If the coefficient of the standard coefficient for the given municipality is higher then the higher one is used.

> then receive 14.3 the basic allocation (see Table 9). So if she was in grade 1, the school would get 14.3×958 = 13,699.4 EUR of funding for this student.

Summary of the Estonian education funding system

The Estonian system has been heavily influenced by the rural character of the country and the political will to keep small schools and small classes. It has also been facing the challenge of two language groups. While the latter led to the separate calculation of funding for Estonian- and Russian-speaking schools, the first challenge and political pressure from small schools led to a system that incentivized the municipalities to keep even very small schools. This might have been hampering the efficiency of the school funding system, and that is why the coefficients (that promoted small schools) were frozen in 2014 and have not since been recalculated on annual bases. This makes the per student income fixed and incentivizes the municipalities to merge schools if possible, and definitely not to create new small schools since they would not get any additional funding for such schools. On the other hand, it is not possible to recommend such a system that is not a sustainable solution in the long term (given the population and structure of population changes over time).

A different case is the funding formula for special needs which is based on the specific class size needs of special needs students. This approach takes effectively into account the teacher time requirement of students and provides sufficient funding for schools in order to create special classes within mainstream education.

Below, we summarize some strengths and weaknesses of the Estonian funding formula. Furthermore, Figure 5 presents the main components of the total allocation to Estonian municipalities.

STRENGTHS	WEAKNESSES
1. Simplicity in terms of calculation; 2. Predictability budgets for municipalities (since the coefficients are fixed); 3. Increased responsibility of the municipality as changes of its expenditure needs per student are not taken into account; 4. Increased motivation for municipalities to close down schools, because coefficient were set per municipality and consolidating the school network does not have an impact on coefficients.	1. Unfair for municipalities with a decline in the number of students (fixed coefficient will not take into account the real expenditure needs) and the other way around; 2. Cognitive/real injustice, today similar municipalities can have very different coefficients as these were calculated years ago (taking into account the situation in the past), which leads to dissatisfaction and makes the system not suitable as a long-term solution.

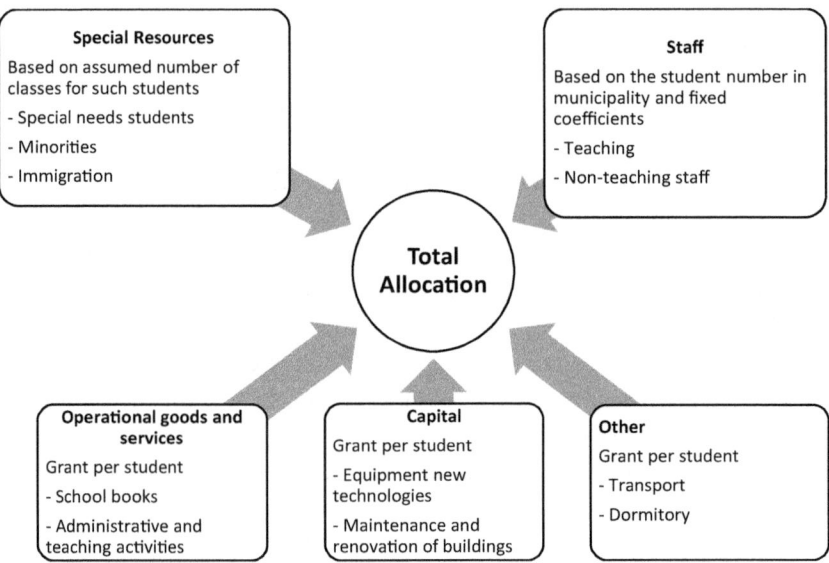

Figure 5: Simplified diagram of the main components of total allocation to municipalities in Estonia; source: Authors.

4.3 Finland

In Finland, the majority of providers of basic and upper secondary level education are run by local authorities or joint municipal consortia (Finnish National Agency for Education, 2017). The funding of basic education is regulated by the Basic Education Act and was reformed in 2010. In this book, we will focus mainly on the situation since this reform. The funding that municipalities receive in order to provide basic education is calculated using the number of school-age children in the municipality for mainstream students, while the funding for special needs students is determined as an estimate for organizing such education which is not based on the actual number of special needs students (Kirjavainen, 2010).

Basic education[31] is provided as a municipal basic service, and local authorities receive statutory government transfers to be used to provide the education. The amount of transfers is calculated based on the number of children aged from 6 to 15 living in the municipality and so-called special

---

31 In Finland, pupils attend comprehensive schools from the age of 7 to the age of 16, which is called basic education, and then they can voluntarily attend upper secondary education in ages 16 to 19.

conditions of the municipality. It is necessary to note that in the end it is the municipalities that democratically decide the exact amount that schools will receive. In contrast to primary education, the numbers of students reported by the schools and the unit prices set by the Finnish Ministry of Education and Culture are used to determine the funding of general upper secondary education and vocational education and training. However, ultimately even this funding is not tied to its use, although the distribution of funding is based on the number of students (Finnish National Agency for Education, 2017).

The general as well as vocational secondary schools are provided mostly by municipalities or the state. The municipalities have two main sources of income (that are then used to fund secondary education): transfers from the central government (including those mentioned to be used for education provision as well as a general allowance, health and social care transfers or culture transfers; the transfer is provided as lump sum) and local taxes. Local councils determine the rate of local income tax and real estate tax. The transfers are calculated using population, some geographical factors and various socio-economic factors (Finnish National Agency for Education, 2017). The description of calculation of these statutory grants is beyond the scope of this book.

Most of the students with special needs are in regular classes. The very much decentralized decision-making system in which municipalities decide about the funding led to a reduction in the number of special schools. Special classes have been founded within mainstream education (as seen below in the case of the Hanko municipality). Besides that, according to the European Agency for Special Needs and Inclusive Education (2017), the Finnish state currently maintains 7 special schools providing comprehensive school education. These are funded in the same way as regular schools.

Below, we provide an explanation of a simplified calculation of the grants from the central government to providers of primary and general and vocational secondary education.

Primary schools

Detailed amounts paid per student
For the year 2017, municipalities received a basic amount of €6,573.54 per pupil aged from 6 to 15 living in the municipality. This basic part of the home allowance is established by the Ministry of Social Affairs and Labor. The special conditions of the municipality then determine some additions to this amount based on the demographics in the municipality such as estimated morbidity, unemployment, number of other than Finnish speaking people, Swedish/

Saame speakers, archipelago area or educational level in the municipality. This supplement is calculated by the Ministry of Finance.

An example of a primary school in a municipality in Finland

In this box, we present an example of a budget of a school in Finland. In principle, the municipality simply follows the state funding. This implies that a primary school with 180 students received funding of 180 × 6,573 = 1,183,140 EUR.

This could be increased by funds for education for students with special needs which is, in general, organized so that these students receive tuition in special groups (classes) within mainstream education. In order to establish these special classes, the school receives €30,351.24 per students with severe developmental disabilities and €18,937,64 per student other than those with severe developmental disabilities.

Secondary schools

The calculation of funding for secondary schools is more complex than in the case of primary education and, for instance, performance indicators are also taken into account.

General upper secondary education
The funding that is transferred to municipalities organizing secondary schools is calculated as the number of students multiplied by the organizer specific unit price of a single student (Saastamoinen and Kortelainen, 2018). The calculation of the unit price for organizer i in year t (P_{it}) can be summarized in the following formula

$$P_{it} = \frac{M_{it} \times N \times P_a}{100}$$

Where P_a is the national average unit price (which is set by the Finnish National Board of Education), N is a national multiplier that smooths out the changes in the average price unit price P_a that might occur because of the differences in organizer specific prices (note that both P_a and N are constant across all organizers). The variation in the unit price for the organizer comes, thus, from the M_{it}. This unit price is determined by the number of students as follows

$$M_{it} = \begin{cases} 100 & \text{if } s_{i,t-1} \geq 200 \\ 100 + 0.4 \times (200 - s_{i,t-1}) & \text{if } 60 \leq s_{i,t-1} < 200 \\ 100 + 0.4 \times (200 - s_{i,t-1}) + 2.1 \times (60 - s_{i,t-1}) & \text{if } 40 \leq s_{i,t-1} < 60 \\ 206 & \text{if } s_{i,t-1} < 40 \end{cases}$$

where $s_{i,t-1}$ is the number of students observed at the beginning of the previous school year. For schools with more than 200 students, no coefficient is applied (M_{it} is 100). Other thresholds are 60 and 40, the multiplier does not increase for schools with fewer than 40 students anymore. Figure 6 shows how the multiplier changes with a change in the number of students. According to Saastamoinen and Kortelainen (2018), the origins of these thresholds are clear from any official documents and are assumed to be set arbitrarily as a result of political negotiations. They nevertheless take into account that average secondary schools in Finland are attended by 100 to 299 students.

It should be noted that basically every municipality needs to add something to the allocation from the central government, and that is a political decision at the municipal level.[32] For all levels of compulsory education, the additional funding from municipalities covers on average 40 to 55 percent of the resources sent to schools. Thus, the differences between the funding per student across municipalities can be relatively large.

Vocational education and training

Vocational education and training is mostly financed from the budget of the Ministry of Education and Culture and is included in the transfers from the central government to local governments (similarly as for primary and general upper secondary education). This funding calculation is mostly based on unit prices multiplied by the number of students and is granted directly to authorized vocational education providers. The providers are then free to spend the money according to their decisions. Currently, the transfers from the central government cover approximately 42 percent of operating costs, and some 58 percent comes from municipalities (Finnish National Board of Education, 2010).

In the calculation of the average unit price, "*the total costs of vocational upper secondary education and training, change in the level of costs as well as changes in the scope and quality of operations due to legislation and other actions by state authorities*" are taken into consideration (Finnish National Board of Education, 2010, p. 23). A unit price of a particular vocational education provider is then based on

---

32 This information was obtained from Prof. Dr. Markku Jahnukainen at the University of Helsinki [email conversation on 7-14/08/2017].

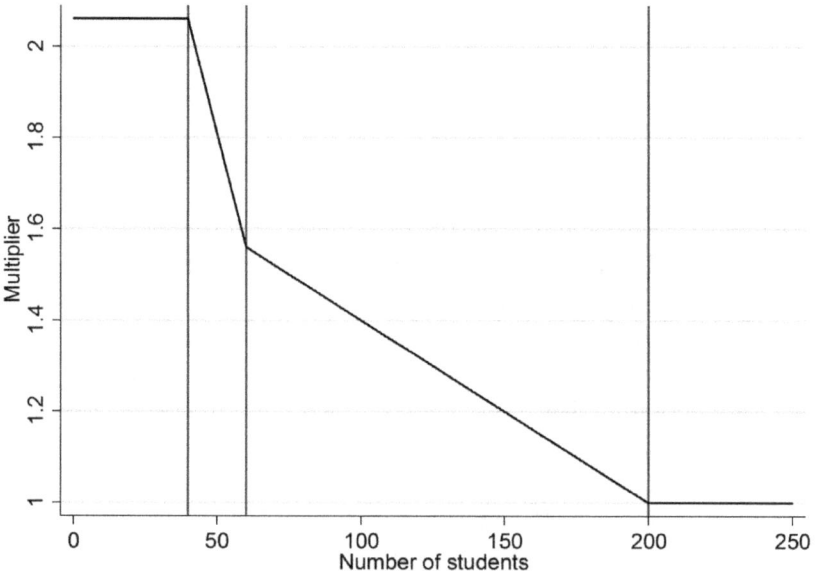

Figure 6: The organizer specific unit price multiplier (divided by 100); source: Saastamoinen and Kortelainen (2018).

"*factors such as the field of education provided, whether the education and training is particularly expensive, the number of students receiving special needs education and the number of students receiving housing from the education institution*" (Finnish National Board of Education, 2010, p. 23). The unit priace of an apprenticeship is approximately 63 percent of the average unit price for vocational education. In Table 10, we summarize the funding model for vocational education.

	Statutory government transfers	Performance-based funding	
		Based on operational outcomes	Based on quality assessment
Vocational upper secondary education and training	unit price / student / year	effectiveness formal teaching qualifications staff development	EFQM excellence model special themes
Apprenticeship training	unit price / student = confirmed apprenticeship agreement / year		EFQM excellence model special themes when necessary

Table 10: Vocational education funding model; source: Finnish National Board of Education (2010).

As seen in the table, as well as the government transfer, there are also performance-based criteria that influence total funding. These criteria are based on operational outcomes determined on the basis of some quantitative indicators and quality assessment. The performance-based funding covers 3 percent of total funding. The quantitative indicators include "*the employment situation of qualification holders, placement in further studies in higher education, drop-out rate, proportion of students passing their qualifications, formal teaching qualifications of the staff and resources allocated towards staff development*" (Finnish National Board of Education, 2010, p. 24).

Calculation of the funding

The average unit price for vocational education was set at EUR 10 278.43 (excluding VAT) in 2017. Due to austerities, the average unit price decreased from 2016 to 2017 by 1.8 percent.

In Table 11, we present the training type-specific unit prices in vocational education. The average unit prices per student in the sectors are obtained by multiplying the unit price in the sector with a sectoral equalization coefficient (equalization coefficient I). Subsequently, all unit prices are adjusted by a general factor of 0.983308.

The funding is then simply calculated by multiplying the number of students in the sector by the adjusted unit price.

Field of study	Unit price	Equalization coefficient	Adjusted unit price
Humanities and education	8,861.97	0.936722	8 301.20
Culture	11 489.55	0.871292	10 010.75
Business administration	7 567.27	0.930568	7 041.86
Natural sciences	8 030.58	0.913317	7 334.47
Technology and transport	10 566.28	0.84926	8 973.52
Natural resources and environment	13 720.56	0.775241	10 636.75
Social services, health and sports	8 320.14	0.941028	7 829.48
Tourism, catering and domestic services	10 101.29	0.872817	8 816.58
In total	10 278.43		

Table 11: The unit prices per training sectors; source: Opetushallitus Utbildningsstyrelsen (2017).

There are also some additional increases for students with special needs.[33] On top of the basic per unit funding, providers that perform better than 80 percent of all eligible providers[34] receive performance-based funding which accounts for 3 percent of total funding. The calculation is as follows:

$$((\text{Performance Index} - 0.928 \text{ min rating}) \times 0.4039490) \times \text{number of students} \times \text{the unit price calculated per training sector} / 1000$$

where 0.928 is the minimum needed to get the performance-based funding and 0.4039490 is so-called price point.[35]

An example of a secondary school in a municipality in Finland

In this box, we present an example of the budget of a school in Hanko. In principle, the municipality simply follows the state funding and adds some additional funds that are needed. Since the figures for 2017 are unavailable, we use the year 2016.

The basic amount per students was 9,075.81 EUR (see https://vos.oph.fi/cgi-bin/tiedot2.cgi?saaja=783;tnimi=vos/v16/v06yt7s16.lis) and the city added on average 3,695 EUR in 2016. So the net effective funding per student in 2016 was 12,770.81 EUR (see https://www.hanko.fi/files/8570/talousarvio2018-2020.pdf, p. 74).

This implies that a general secondary school with 180 students received funding of 180 × 12,770.81 = 2,298,745.80 EUR.

Special needs schools

Since 2011, special needs students have generally not received any special funding. The funding for most students is already included in the basic allocation. The only exception is a small group of students within Tier 3. For these purposes, the Finnish system distinguishes between two types of additional funding for extended education: i) students with severe developmental disabilities and ii) students other than those with severe developmental disabilities. For the first group, the municipalities receive the basic allocation

---

33   For details we refer to http://oph.fi/download/187736_opetus_ja_kulttuuritoimen_rahoitus_2017.pdf.
34   Note that not all providers can receive this funding; they must be big enough to get reliable statistical data and the funding is limited to some study fields.
35   Details of its calculation are provided again in http://oph.fi/download/187736_opetus_ja_kulttuuritoimen_rahoitus_2017.pdf.

amount multiplied by the coefficient 4.76 (i.e. €30,351.24 per student in 2017). For the latter group, the municipalities receive additional funding equal to the basic amount multiplied by the coefficient of 2.97 (i.e. € 18,937.64 per student in 2017). Funding for these students is decided on an individual basis and these funds are often used to pay for, for example, educational assistants.

In the following chapter, we will describe how the funds received by a municipality from the central government are further allocated to the schools. It should be noted that basically every municipality needs to add something to the allocation from central government and that it is a political decision at the municipal level.[36]

The case of the municipality of Hanko[37]

As a case study for Finland, we have chosen the municipality of Hanko as it faces the challenge of two language groups (Finnish and Swedish speakers). As in the majority of Finnish municipalities, the state funding is not enough to finance education, so the city council decides annually on the (additional) budget resources. In Hanko, there are 53.5 percent of Finnish and 43.7 of Swedish speakers. Within the basic education, there are 6 schools that provide instruction in Finnish and 6 in Swedish.

The funding formula in Hanko is kept relatively simple and is based on the number of students in the given school. It largely follows the amounts determined by the central government. Thus, the amount that a school obtains per student is determined by the level of education. The schools receive fixed amount of €6,573 per student in elementary education and €10,275 in secondary education.

The funds for education have been budgeted to enable the education for pupils with special needs to be organized so that these students receive classes in special groups (classes). These special groups are administered by a special school and its principal. In order to establish these special classes that require more teachers and (educational) assistants, the school receives €30,351.24 per student with severe developmental disabilities and €18,937,64 per student other than students with severe developmental disabilities. These funds are paid to the school based on the number of enrolled students at the beginning of the academic year.

---

36 This information was obtained from Prof. Dr. Markku Jahnukainen at the University of Helsinki [email conversation on 7-14/08/2017].
37 The funding system was described by Mr. Karl-Erik Gustafsson, Head of Education Department of the municipality of Hanko [email conversation on 10-13/08/2017].

> **An example of a school in a municipality in Finland**
>
> In this box, we present an example of the budget of a school in Finland. In principle, the municipality simply follows the state funding. This implies that a primary school with 180 students received a funding of 180 × 6,573 = 1,183,140 EUR.
>
> This could be increased by funds for education for students with special needs which is, in general, organized so that these students receive classes in special groups (classes) within mainstream education. In order to establish these special classes, the school receives €30,351.24 per student with severe developmental disabilities and €18,937,64 per student other than students with severe developmental disabilities.

Summary of the Finnish education funding system

Finnish education as well as the education funding system is very much decentralized with a large share of decision-making in the hands of the municipalities. Figure 7 shows the main sources of the allocation from central government and municipalities to Finnish schools.

In such a system where municipalities receive funds on a per citizen of school age basis and only relatively a very limited share of students receive further support leads to a reduction in the number of special schools, and more often the inclusion of special needs students into mainstream educational institutions. This is further strengthened by the fact that the basic allocation already includes funding for most special needs students.

Since the allocation does not depend on the number of classes or similar factors, the municipalities have little incentive to further promote or create small schools that would make the provision costlier and less efficient. In the municipality of Hanko, they mostly follow the national system of funding and fund schools based on the per student formula. The funding for special needs students is directly paid to the schools, which makes them responsible and able to establish classes for special needs students within mainstream schools. Even students in intensified support (Tier 2) often study in special small groups although this has not been the aim. These students should mainly study in mainstream classes/groups in accordance with inclusion principles.

Below, we summarize some strengths and weaknesses of the Finnish funding formula.

STRENGTHS	WEAKNESSES
1. Large flexibility and responsibility given to municipalities that can democratically decide on the level of funding as well as on the policy preferences in spending; 2. Focus on outcomes (self-evaluation of schools and teachers) instead of inputs; 3. Disincentivize over-identification as a large share of special needs students are included in the basic allocation; 4. Very equitable system since primary schools have to accept students and they provide lunches and text books for free to all students.	1. Municipalities have often to co-fund schools from their budgets and local taxes; 2. Since schools are in large part co-funded by municipalities, there are larger differences in the level of funding that is provided to schools among municipalities which would not be the case were the schools funded mostly directly by the state; 3. Little or no extra support for gifted students; 4. The additional funding for small general secondary school may disincentives merges etc.

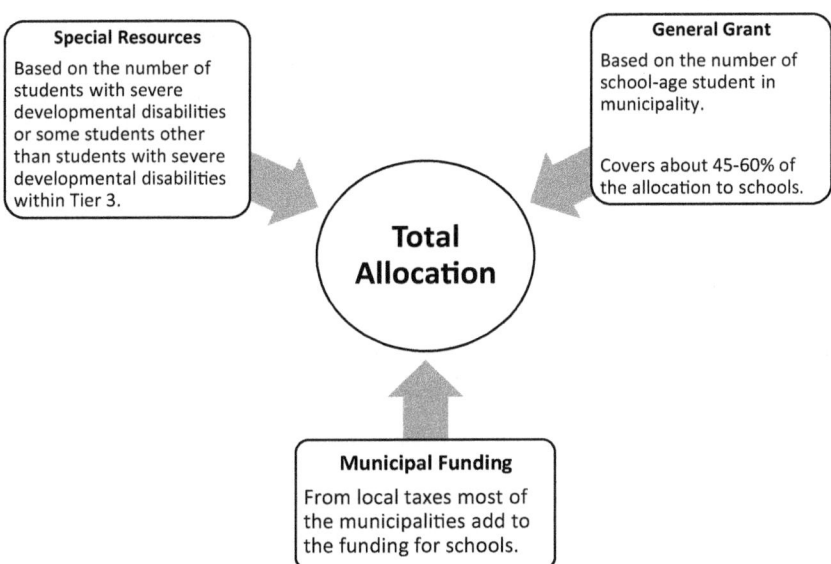

Figure 7: Simplified diagram of the main sources allocated to schools in Finland; source: Authors.

4.4 Flanders

Unlike in the other regions studied in the book, it is primary and secondary school boards that receive funding from the Flemish Community, and not strictly geographically determined areas such as municipalities or districts. A new funding formula for operating expenses in primary and secondary schools was introduced in 2008/09. In addition, a new mechanism for allocating teaching staff in primary education was implemented in 2012/2013. In the following part, we describe important parts of this funding formula before the funding for special needs students – which has recently been reformed – is discussed in detail.

Primary schools

The funding for primary schools consists of funding for staff (including teaching staff, replacement units for teachers' absences, school principals) and operations budgets.

Staff funding
The funding of teaching hours for primary schools in Flanders is mainly based on the number of students and certain point envelopes. The staff formation of the schools consists of teaching hours, other hours, points and replacement units. Teaching hours can be used to appoint teaching staff. Other hours can be used to appoint paramedical staff. Each of the point envelopes is in turn used for staff and support members. The replacement units are used to fill short absences of personnel. Finally, every school is entitled to hire a principal (if a school has fewer than 180 pupils, the principal also has a part-time teaching assignment).

Teaching staff funding
The basic framework of primary schools' financing is comprised of the teaching hours according to the scales, SES-teaching hours and additional teaching hours.

In primary education, the basic framework for staff funding can be used to appoint teachers, physical education teachers and teachers for ideological courses. Conversion from the basic framework funding to financed or subsidized full-time jobs of teachers or physical education teachers and teachers of ideological courses is done by dividing the teaching hours by 24. The quotient is equal to the number of possible full-time jobs to be funded.

Teaching hours according to the scales
The regular students are counted to determine teaching hours according to the scales. Afterwards they are separated into categories and weighted based on several characteristics. Students in primary schools that are situated in Brussels receive a weighting coefficient of 1.11, students in schools that are situated in a community with a population density of fewer than 100 inhabitants

per square meter have a weight of 1.05 and students that live in a center for child care and family support, or have been living outside their own family, receive a weighting coefficient of 1.5. For other students, the coefficient is 1. These coefficients are multiplicative. A student living outside his/her family and going to school in Brussels is as such weighed at 1.665 (1.5 × 1.11). The number of students is then rounded up. In schools with multiple locations, the count can be separate or together depending on the distance between the locations. There is one common scale for all primary schools (Appendix A of "Lestijdenschaal gewoon basisonderwijs"). It shows the number of teaching hours the school receives based on the number of weighted students. On the teaching hours generated by these scales, an SES-percentage of 97.16 is subsequently applied. The result of this calculation is rounded. Schools that are not entitled to at least 26 teaching hours according to these scales receive 26 teaching hours.

SES-teaching hours
Socio-economic status teaching hours are allocated to schools based on the socio-economic status of students. This status is assessed based on several student characteristic indicators. Each indicator represents an aspect of the socio-economic status; the indicators are the following:
1. Whether or not the mother finished secondary education is used to indicate the cultural baggage and the social capital of the family and the student.
2. Whether or not the student receives an educational grant is used to indicate the financial situation of the family.
3. Whether or not the language spoken in the family differs from the instruction language in the given school[38] is used as an indicator for both cultural and linguistic capital of the family.

For each student that ticks off at least one indicator, the school receives SES-teaching hours. For the educational level of the mother the school receives 0.26710 teaching hours; for language spoken in the family this is 0.29116 and for educational grant 0.11917. The additional hours are cumulative per student. A student whose family language is not Dutch and whose mother did not finish secondary education gives the school 0.29116 + 0.26710 additional teaching hours. The SES-teaching hours a school receives are meant to be

---

38   The language the student speaks at home is not the instruction language, where the student speaks with no member of the family or, in a family of three people, with at most one family member in the instruction language.

used to limit the impact of the socio-economic status on the outcomes of the students.

Additional teaching hours according to the scales
Every school where the average number of students per full-time teacher is higher than 18.5 receives additional teaching hours to stay below this student-teacher ratio.

To be entitled to additional teaching hours the result of the $24 \times A / B$ division should be higher than 18.5, where A is the number of regular students in school on the counting day and B is the sum of the teaching hours according to the scales of the school and the SES-teaching hours for the school, both for the current school year. The result of this division equals the number of students per full-time teacher. The number of additional teaching hours is the difference between C and B rounded up, where C is $(24 \times A / B) / 18.5$. These additional hours make sure the student/teacher ratio almost equals 18.5 in primary schools, for which this number would be higher without the correction mechanism.

Complementary teaching hours
On top of the basic framework, there are complementary teaching hours. These hours are subsidized or financed with regard to religion, ethics, and culture on the one hand and for non-Dutch-speaking newcomers on the other hand.

For courses in acknowledged religions and ethics, two teaching hours per group of students are financed on top of the basic framework. In subsidized free schools that provide neither religion nor ethics, two hours of cultural education are financed. The number of courses and of teaching hours for the most followed course is determined (Appendix C "Calculation of the most followed course religion, ethics or cultural education"; Vlaamse Overheid, 2005). After the distribution of the teaching hours for the most followed courses, those for the less followed courses are calculated. The number of complementary hours per student group contains as many teaching hours as the most followed course. Starting from 10 students, a lesser followed course can be split up into multiples of 5 students when the corresponding student group of the most followed course also splits up.

To be entitled to the complementary teaching hours for non-Dutch-speaking newcomers the school needs to organize a plan of action for each individual newcomer. This plan of action has to provide both study elements and study evolution. They also need to have an adequate number of newcomers. For schools with only one location the school needs at least 4 non-Dutch-speaking newcomers. For all other schools the minimum is set at 6 newcomers. When the number of newcomers is counted at the school community level, a minimum of 12 newcomers is needed. When this number of newcomers is met, the school receives 2 additional teaching hours and 1.5 additional hours per newcomer (Vlaamse Overheid, 2006).

Supplementary teaching hours
A final component of the basic framework consists of the supplementary teaching hours for a voluntary merger and the supplementary teaching hours for temporary home education. When a voluntary merger takes place, a school is entitled to supplementary teaching hours in order to spread the potential negative effects of the merger over time. The number of supplementary teaching hours depends on the following elements:
– The teaching hours package based on the regulations assuming the original structure of the school remains unchanged and the teaching hours package is based on the new structure after the fusion.
– The difference between the two packages is weighted based on the year (100 percent in the year of the merger, 75 percent one year later, 50 percent 2 years later and 25 percent three years after the merger) and this number of supplementary teaching hours is awarded to the school.

These hours can, however, only be used to acquire temporary personnel.
In certain circumstances students are entitled to temporary home education. The student is entitled to this only when the nature of the condition is severe, the parents request home education and one of the locations of the school is more than 10 kilometers away. When all of these conditions are met 4 supplementary teaching hours per week per student are financed or subsidized (Vlaamse Overheid, 1997).

Special pedagogic assignments (SPA)
Up to 3 percent of the teaching hours package awarded can be reserved for pedagogic assignments. This maximum can be exceeded as long as the local committee regarding working conditions grants permission.
The teaching hours that can be used for these special pedagogic assignments are called SPA hours (BPT in Dutch) and are aimed at optimizing the pedagogic-didactic organization. An example is assigning certain coordination assignments to personnel.

Point envelope
'Point envelopes' allow schools to hire employees as support and staff members. The three offices that can be filled by using these points are care

coordinator, ICT-coordinator and administrative employee. On top of the three-point envelopes corresponding to these offices, there is one additional envelope to support the school community.

The point envelopes for care and ICT are calculated per school based on the number of students. While every school receives a point envelope for ICT, a school can use the points only if it is part of a school community. A total point envelope is distributed over all students. In 2016 this yielded a point value of 0.03969 per student. Schools that are in a school community can use these points to acquire ICT-coordinators. For the care point envelope, there is no such condition and points are distributed based on the number of students (see Appendix "Puntenenveloppe zorgbeleid"; Vlaamse Overheid, 2005).

The point envelope for administrative services is also based on a 0.1543 point value per student in community education and a 0.1745 point value per student in subsidized education, with a minimum of 9 points per school.

On top of these point envelopes, the school board is also entitled to a stimulus envelope to support the operational expenses. This point envelope is free to spend over all three of the previously mentioned domains and separate functions to support the school community. Schools are also allowed to give up to 10 percent of their ICT and administrative support points to the school board (Vlaamse Overheid, 2005).

The points from the point envelopes can be converted into the following positions: chief coordinator of the school community and/or staff members of the school community. Points assigned to a school for the care envelope can be used only to appoint care coordinators. The same is true for ICT coordinators from the ICT point envelope and administrative employees from the administrative support envelope.

The price of a position is expressed in a point weight. Depending on the position and educational level of the applicant, the point value varies for a full-time position. The number of hours for which he or she is appointed influences the number of points needed (see Appendix "Het puntengewicht van een betrekking" for details; Vlaamse Overheid, 2005).

Replacement units
Replacement units are additional teaching hours that can be used only to cover short absences of employees for which there are no alternative compensation measures. Short absences are those absences for which no other replacement can be financed or subsidized under another regulation. These replacement units are only awarded when there is no replacement for 10-day absences, pregnancy leave etc. The replacement units can be used to appoint temporary personnel in order to replace absent employees. Replacement units can only

be used when combined at the level of a cooperation platform in which there is a covenant.

The number of replacement units is equal to the replacement coefficient X, the total number of teaching hours of the school in the previous school year. In 2015-2016 the replacement coefficient was set at 56.73054954. The total number of teaching hours is then given as the sum of all teaching hours of the basic framework. Appointing an employee with these replacement units is done as follows: X × number of appointed days / 7 = Y, where X is the assignment on a weekly basis of the staff being replaced, expressed in 10.000th's and Y the needed replacement units. To appoint someone in a full-time assignment this is always approximately 1.429 units per day (Vlaamse Overheid, 2005).

The School Principal funding

Every school receives funding for the office of principal, regardless of size. In schools with fewer than 180 students, the principal also has to teach between 4 and 14 hours depending on the school size. The principal has a teaching assignment of 14 teaching hours in schools with fewer than 20 students, 10 teaching hours in schools with between 20 and 129 students and 4 teaching hours in schools with 130 to 179 students. For schools with more than 180 students the principal is free of a teaching assignment.

In the Brussels Capital Region, these teaching assignments for school principals are different. It is 14 teaching hours in schools with fewer than 20 students, 10 teaching hours in schools with between 20 and 69 students and 4 teaching hours in schools with 70 to 99 students. Here, principals of schools with more than 100 students do not receive a teaching assignment. Depending on the respective point envelopes, the teaching assignment can be converted into an ICT or care assignment or the principal can fulfill a staff membership position in the school community. In schools formed out of a voluntary fusion, funding can also be provided for the position of assistant principal when several conditions are met. This person too has to fulfill a teaching assignment in certain conditions[39] (Vlaamse Overheid, 2005).

Operations budgets

The financing of operations is based on objective differences, student characteristics and school characteristics (Groenez, Juchtmans, Smet, & Stevens, 2015).

---

39 More information can be found in the circular "Personeelsformatie scholen in het gewoon basisonderwijs."

Objective differences
The objective differences are based on the principles of neutrality and world-view. As only Communal Education (GO!) is constitutionally obliged to provide neutral education, it is entitled to compensation. This compensation is set at 3 percent of the indexed distributable means for students of these schools. Comparably, as only communal (GO!) and officially subsidized education (OGO) are obliged to provide multiple world-view orienting courses, these schools receive additional funding. The objective difference for world-view was set at 4.5 percent of the indexed distributable means of these schools. The quantification of the compensation for these objective differences was based on a consulting report regarding the income and expenditure of Flemish schools (Deloitte & Touche, 2001).

The ratios for neutrality of 3 percent and of ethics courses of 4.5 percent are used to calculate the amount of money that school boards that are entitled to these funds receive per student. The total amount per student for neutral education is equal to:

indexed distributable means × 0.03 / (the total number of students + the number of students per objective difference × 0.03)

in the case of neutral education and in cases of ethics courses 0.045 replaces 0.03, otherwise the formula stays the same (AGODI, 2016; Vlaamse Overheid, 1998).

Student characteristics
The second element that decides the operations budget of primary school boards is the composition of student characteristics in these schools. The four indicators to measure the student characteristics are educational level of the mother, educational grant, mother tongue and neighborhood. The goal of these characteristics is to map the social environment in which the students grew up. Every year a percentage of the educational budget for primary education is set aside to compensate for student characteristics. As of 2016 this percentage will rise from 14.5625 to 15.5 in 2020. This budget is then for primary education equally distributed across the four indicators. Afterwards the budget per indicator is divided by the number of relevant students. The values of the different characteristics are then summed up at the school level. One remark is that there is a correction when schools have a very large number of students scoring on a certain indicator. The additional financing is calculated for a maximum of the mean percentage of students scoring on a characteristic increased with two standard deviations.

A student can have multiple student characteristics. In this case, the school board receives the sum of the generated amounts.

School characteristics

The third element to decide the operations budget is school characteristics. In primary education, this is the only difference between mainstream and special needs education. The point value per primary school student is set to 8.[40]

Point envelope ICT

Another source of income is the financing of ICT operations. These are based on the weighted number of students (1,25 times the number of students) and multiplied by a budgetary coefficient of 0.7163. A school with 200 students would as such receive 200 × 1.25 × 0.7163 = 179.08 EUR. These resources can only be used for logistical and material support of ICT coordination.

Calculation of allocations

After computing the points for each and approving the final budget, the school boards receive allocations proportionally according to their points.

An example of a primary school board budget in Flanders

In Flanders, the school board receives the funding, and then distributes it to the schools it governs. Therefore, in this box, we present an example of the budget of a Flemish provincial school board (OGO). The calculation follows the funding formula described above. In this example, we take a primary school with 180 students. To make the example more interesting, we assume that 20 students come from a non-Dutch-speaking family, 10 receive educational grants and 5 come from the travelling population (such as Roma people).

The total allocation is composed of staff and operating budget.

Staff formation
The staff funding consists of principal funding, teaching staff and point envelopes. Since the school has 180 students, it receives a fully funded principal without a teaching assignment.

The funding of teaching staff is determined as 175 × 1 + 5 × 1.5 = 182.5 teaching hours. The 5 students are the Roma students that are weighted by 1.5. According to the table from Appendix 2 of the Basic Education Law (http://data-onderwijs.vlaanderen.be/documenten/bestand.ashx?nr=5100), this weighted number of students generates 236 teaching

---

40   For nursery schools (2.5 to 6 years), the point value is 6.

hours. And then a coefficient of 0.9716 is applied, yielding the final number of teaching hours: 229. By diving this number of teaching hours, we receive 9.5 full-time equivalent positions.

Furthermore, the school board would receive some complementary teaching hours based on the religion of its students. This is determined by paragraph 3.2.1.3 in the circular on Staff Formation in Mainstream Primary Schools (http://data-onderwijs.vlaanderen.be/edulex/document.aspx?docid=13615#3-2-1-3). Assuming that the majority of students would opt for non-confessional ethics (about 100 students), 60 for Christianity and 20 Muslim, the school board would get 12 complementary hours and approximately 4 and 2 hours for Christian and Muslim teaching complementary hours.

Lastly, the school board would receive $180 \times 1.25 \times 0.03969 = 8.93$ points for ICT and $180 \times 01543 = 27.77$ points for administration. The exact specification of who can be hired based on these points is given in the same circular at paragraph 1.4.1.3 (see http://data-onderwijs.vlaanderen.be/edulex/document.aspx?docid=13641#1-4-1-3).

Operating budget
The school board receives funding for objective difference, student characteristics, school characteristics and point envelope for ICT.

Since community schools are required to teach religiously neutral education, they are entitled to compensation for objective differences. The funding per students is, consequently, in the end increased by 4.5 percent. In our case, this would be approximately $(116,234.22+3,694.1+161.17) \times 0.045 = 5,404.02$ EUR.

The additional funding based on student characteristics is calculated as 15 percent of the total budget for primary schools, divided by 4 and then distributed equally among the 4 categories (low educational level of the mother, receiver of a school grant, non-Dutch home language and living in a poor neighborhood). In 2017, the funding per non-Dutch home language was 128.66 EUR and the funding per student receiving educational grants was 112.09 EUR. So it is $128.66 \times 20 = 2,573.20$ EUR for non-Dutch home language students and $112.09 \times 10 = 1,120.90$ EUR for students receiving educational grants. In total, the student characteristics funding was 3,694.1 EUR.

Since we assume a primary school board, the points for school characteristics are computed as follows $180 \times 8 = 1,440$ points. In 2017, one point was equivalent to 80.72 EUR, thus, the total funding for our school board would be 116,234.22 EUR (equivalent to 645.75 EUR per student).

And, lastly, the school board receives funds for ICT operating budgets. These are calculated as 180 × 1.25 × 0.7163 = 161.17 EUR and can only be used for logistic and material support of ICT coordination.

Area	Allocations in positions, hours, points and euros
Staff information	
– School principal	1 position without teaching obligations
– Teaching staff	9.5 full-time eq. positions
– Complementary teaching hours	18 teaching hours
– Point envelope	8.93 points for ICT + 27.77 points for administration
Operating budgets	
– School characteristisc	116,234.22 EUR
– Objective differences	Approximately 5,404.02 EUR
– Student characteristisc	3,694.1 EUR
– ICT operating budget	161.17 EUR

Table 12: Allocations to a Flemish community school board; source: Authors.

The funding for this model school board is summarized in Table 12. For staff formation, it would receive funding for a principal, 9.5 full-time equivalent positions for teaching staff, 18 teaching hours for teaching religion, 8.93 points for ICT and 27.77 points for administration. The funding from the points (such as for school characteristics) is calculated proportionally according to the points that school boards receive from the overall remaining budget for all school boards (i.e. if there were 2 school boards with 100 and 200 points, respectively, the first would receive 1/3 of the remaining budget and the second one 2/3). For operating budgets, it would receive 135,493.51 EUR which mostly comes from the funding for school characteristics.

The school boards then usually simply split the total budget (after putting some part aside as a reserve) according to the number of students in each school (if a school board manages more than one school). Note that these decisions are in the hands of school principals and can differ significantly across school boards.

Secondary schools

Like that for primary schools, the funding for secondary schools consists of funding for staff and operations budgets.

Staff funding
Staff funding for secondary schools is mainly based on the number of students and point envelopes.

Teaching hours
In secondary education, the basic framework for staff funding can be used to appoint teachers, physical education teachers and teachers for ideological courses. The conversion from the basic framework funding to financed or subsidized full-time jobs of teachers or physical education teachers and teachers for ideological courses is different from the conversion used for primary schools. There are 3 conversion rates depending on the year of secondary education – specifically, the conversion is done by dividing the teaching hours by 22 (for years 1-2 of secondary), 21 (for years 3-4), and 20 hours (for years 5-6).[41] The quotient thus obtained then represents the number of funded full-time jobs.

Secular courses
The number of teacher hours a school receives is based on the number of weekly teacher hours per student. This individual number of teacher hours is calculated based on certain coefficients depending on field of study, type and level of education (see Appendix "The types of education classes" and Appendix "Overview of the coefficients for teaching hours per student"; Vlaamse Overheid, 1998). The coefficients are largest for a first bracket of students. As the number of students increases, these students are placed in a higher bracket. The marginal coefficient diminishes per bracket. In a school with 80 students in the second and third cycles of general secondary education the first 25 students have a coefficient of 1.90. The second bracket of 26-50 students receives a coefficient of 1.70 and for students 51-81 a coefficient of 1.60 is set. The result of this method is then corrected by multiplication with a coefficient of 0.9657. The resulting teacher hours are then rounded.

For certain schools, other, so-called minimal packages regulations are in place. The assignment of these minimal packages is done based on articles regarding rationalization norms as set out in the "Codex Secundair Onderwijs". For these schools the coefficients are replaced by a minimal package. This adaptation is possible only for schools that meet the following criteria such as
- The replacement scheme provides a more advantageous result for the school than the standard calculation based on the coefficients.

---

41 The exceptions such as teaching practical classes in vocational education may involve up to 30 hours.

- The number of teacher hours to which the school is entitled according to the minimum-package scheme divided by the number of tenable teacher hours at 100 percent is greater than or equal to 15 percent.
- The number of teacher hours granted via the coefficient regulation divided by the number of teacher hours to which the school is entitled according to the minimum package scheme is less than or equal to 85 percent.

For general and technical secondary education with a component for professional sports, students with a professional athlete statute A are not taken into account for the coefficient ruling, but 2.9 teacher hours are granted to the school per student. Pupils with a top sport status of B are counted as regular pupils. There are also exceptions for other athlete and gardening schools. For instance, for pupils with a top-level sports certificate B and A, a flat-rate package of 20 teacher hours is awarded to the school per academic year in a maximum of one of the two forms of education (ASO or TSO) if this is more advantageous than the result of the coefficient calculation. These teacher hours can only be used for the organization of top sports. A separate structure was also designed for land and horticultural schools. Depending on the number of pupils, they can claim 29, 58 or 87 teaching hours. The personnel who are appointed from here are responsible for the operation and maintenance of the cultures, the greenhouses and the livestock and giving demonstrations during practical lessons. The number of teacher hours obtained with this calculation is multiplied by the application rate for minimum packages of 98.57%. This result is then rounded.

Religion, non-confessional morals, cultural ethics and own culture and religion
There are also hours allocated to teaching religion, non-confessional morals, cultural ethics and own culture and religion (for details, see http://data-onderwijs.vlaanderen.be/edulex/document.aspx?docid=12997 Section 3.2.2). These are allocated using so-called slitting norms which are applied at the level of individual learning cycles and depend on the curriculum. In the first year of the A stream[42] and the second year of the first cycle[43] of secondary

---

[42] The so-called B stream is intended for students who have not obtained a certificate of primary education, have a learning deficiency or are less suitable for predominantly theoretical education. After one year in the B stream, such students can transfer to the A stream
[43] Here, a cycle means 2 years of education and there are 3 cycles in secondary schools (6 years in total).

education, the norms are: 26 students for 2 classes, 51 for 3 classes, 76 for 4 classes etc. (Vlaamse Overheid, 1998). The standards assume fewer students per class in the B stream or vocational training.

To determine the number of classes in non-confessional morals and religion in the official schools and the number of classes for these courses and cultural ethics and own culture and religion in subsidized free non-confessional education the distribution is 10 students for 2 classes, 21 for 3 classes, 28 for 4 classes, etc. at 7 students per class.

The number of classes is then multiplied by the weekly teaching hours for the corresponding courses. Next the calculated number of teacher hours is multiplied by a coefficient of 0.98. These hours need to be used for the corresponding courses. They can be used both for teaching hours and non-teaching hours, with regard to the course.

Special pedagogic assignments
Up to 3% of the total usable teacher hours can be reserved for special pedagogic assignments. These cannot be: teacher hours for full-time vocational secondary education on a modular system and teacher hours for athletics schools (Vlaamse Overheid, 2014).

Plage hours
'Plage hours' are teaching hours that a teacher performs above the minimum and below the maximum of a full-time position. These numbers are specified for all positions in education (Vlaamse Overheid, 1998). Outside the financed and subsidized hours, teachers cannot be asked to teach additional hours. Only one plage hour can be assigned. Staff members can only be awarded plage hours when these hours are necessary for organizational reasons and when they are organized in a transparent and equal way.

Schools belonging to a school community can organize a maximum of 1.3 percent of the sum of the teaching hour packages within the community as plage hours. To facilitate the reduction of plage hours, 20,000 hours are distributed across all school communities, proportional to their share in the total teaching hour package. For schools that do not belong to a school community on top of the 3% rule there is a rule that the percentage of plage hours cannot be higher than that of the 2001-2002 school year.

Transfer teaching hours
Teaching hours can be transferred to the next school year or to another school. To transfer to the next school year there is a maximum of 2% of the number of usable teacher hours. Teacher hours that are the result of conversions of

points cannot be counted for this calculation. The transferred hours can only be used in the next school year. There is no limit on the number of hours that can be transferred to other schools (Vlaamse Overheid, 1998).

Long-term illness
When students are ill for a longer period home education can be provided. During the long-term illness the government provides 4 supplementary hours per student per week.

School communities
Schools that do not belong to a school community receive an increase of the calculated teaching hours, including usage percentages, of 1 %. The goal of these means is to reduce the number of organizable plage hours and to reduce pressure of work.

Schools that are part of a school community enjoy a beneficial calculation of the point envelopes and the staff of these schools can be used in a broader sense. Members of staff and supporting personnel can be put to work for the totality of the school community. Supporting personnel can be used for assignments for other schools in the same community.

Welcoming education
Welcoming education for non-Dutch-speaking newcomers consists of a welcoming year and support, counseling and the follow-up of these newcomers. Also building expertise related to former non-Dutch-speaking newcomers in regular secondary education is a part of this educational type. As these forms of counseling and support are expensive, additional specific teacher hours are awarded. These hours are awarded to the school community. When a school does not belong to a community it receives the hours itself.

Non-Dutch-speaking newcomers are those children between 12 and 18 years old that have stayed in Belgium for at most 1 year without interruption, that do not have Dutch as their home language and do not know the language well enough to follow classes. Finally, these students may not have been registered in a school where Dutch is the teaching language for more than 9 months.

A specific teaching hours package is provided for welcoming education. These hours cannot be used for any purpose other than welcoming education. Every school with welcoming education receives 2.5 teacher hours per regular non-Dutch-speaking newcomer in the welcoming year. On top of these hours, the schools receive an additional 0.9 teacher hours for non-Dutch-speaking newcomers in the previous year. These hours can only be used to guide, support and follow up former welcomed students in regular education. For calculation purposes the point weight of a newcomer equals 16.

Equal educational opportunity means-GOK
As an extension to the package of teacher hours, extra teacher hours are also provided for equal educational opportunities and disadvantaged students. The GOK decree or the decree for equal educational chances bundled together all the initiatives regarding this subject. The goal of this policy is to reduce educational backlogs of disadvantaged native and foreign students. In order to meet this goal, this target group should receive additional teacher hours, support and guidance (Blaton, 2008). Just as with the SES means in primary education, the target students are discovered by several indicators. In order to benefit from the program and receive extra teacher hours a school needs a minimum of 10% weighted disadvantaged students in the first cycle and a minimum of 25% weighted disadvantaged students in the second and third cycles.

There are 5 equal opportunities indicators specified in the decree. To each of these indicators a weight, expressed in points, is assigned. Below are the 5 indicators with their respective point-values. The indicator school grant has 2 point values, one for students that only indicate this indicator and one (potentially together with non-Dutch home speakers) for those that indicate at least one other as well.

1. Parents belong to the traveling population (Roma, circus etc.) This indicator has a weight coefficient of 0.8 points.
2. The mother does not have a degree of secondary education. This indicator has a weight coefficient of 0.6 points.
3. The student is temporarily or permanently accommodated admitted outside the family. This indicator has a value of 0.8 points.
4. The family receives one or more school grants. If this is the only indicator checked the point value is 0.4. This weight is however corrected as the number of students that meet this requirement is multiplied by 0.4417. This brings the real point value to 0.17668. When the student also qualifies for another indicator the weight is set at 0.18 points.
5. The language the student speaks at home is not Dutch. This indicator has a weight coefficient of 0.2 points. For students that meet multiple indicators the weights are cumulative up to a maximum of 1.2 points per student.

The weight coefficient of 0.4417 for school grants also counts toward the count of weighted disadvantaged students. All other indicators are weighted as one in this regard. This calculation happens at the school level. Afterwards the points generated in the first cycle are added up and multiplied by 1.5 when the school is in the Brussels Capital Region or if the school has more than 55% disadvantaged students. If the school meets both criteria the multiplication happens twice. The total number of points is multiplied by 0.2916 teacher hours.

The point values of students in the second and third grades are also summarized. This value is then multiplied by 1.5 when the school is in the Brussels Capital Region or if the school has more than 55% disadvantaged students. If the school meets both criteria the multiplication happens twice. The total number of points is multiplied by 0.1225 teacher hours.

A school receives the sum of these teacher hour students only if the result over all cycles yields 6 extra teacher hours or more. The calculation happens every 3 years (GOK period) and during this period the additional hours remain the same. The extra teacher hours can be used across cycles as long as they aim to improve equal educational outcomes.

The School Principal funding
A full-time principal's position is assigned to a school with at least 83 regular students on the counting day. For schools that organize only a first (years 1 to 2) or a first and second cycle (years 1 to 4), a minimum of 120 students is required for eligibility for this full-time position. When the number of students is lower, the principal is also assigned some teaching. This assignment consists of a half-time teaching assignment, minus four teaching hours (Vlaamse Overheid, 1998).

Global point envelope
Next to the teacher hours package, there is also a global point envelope. This point envelope provides a school board with means to hire supporting staff and staff members (with the exception of a principal) at the school level. This envelope also tries to provide a policy with regard to task and function differentiation. Below we show the calculations of these points. The points can then be used to appoint staff members, supporting staff and teaching staff within the area of task and function differentiation. Employees can also be promoted to a higher pay scale in a supporting position and made class free. For schools that are part of a school community, this community receives the point envelope. The community then divides the points according to its own calculations based on agreed upon criteria. Schools that do not belong to a community receive the funds directly. For all points mentioned below a weight coefficient of 96.57% is in place.

Global point envelope awarded to the school community
1. Each secondary school receives 120 points if it has at least 600 regular students. Schools also receive 120 points for every addtional 600 enrolled students.
2. Each secondary school receives 120 points if it has at least 300 special needs students. Schools also receive 120 points for every additional 600 enrolled special needs students.
3. Additional points are awarded for schools with practical courses: 120 points when 7 full-time teachers taught practical courses in the previous year and are teaching at least 6 in the next. An additional multiple of 120 points is awarded if the number of teachers for practical courses is 15 and 14 (240 points), 19 and 18 (360 points), 22 and 21 (480 points), 29 and 28 (600 points), 31 and 30 respectively (720 points), 33 and 32 (840 points), 36 and 35 (960 points), 43 and 41 (1080 points), and so on for each multiple of 7 and 6.
4. 120 points are awarded to each special needs secondary school if the total number of weekly teaching hours organized as vocational training or practical courses in that school is at least 210. An additional 120 points are awarded per multiple of 210 weekly teaching hours organized as this type of course.
5. School communities can aggregate teaching hours/positions to reach the minimum demanded in point 3.
6. Additional points to be used for supporting staff are the following:
   - Students entitled to additional teacher hours GOK funding multiplied by 0.2971.
   - Other students multiplied by 0.2851.
   - Weekly teacher hours for schools that are entitled to GOK funding multiplied by 0.3025.
   - Other school teacher hours multiplied by 0.2902.
   - 82 points are awarded to each extraordinary school and on top of that schools receive additional points depending on students' weight coefficients.[44]
7. Points awarded for function and task differentiation.
   - The number of mainstream students is multiplied by 0.02316074.
   - Weekly package teaching hours are multiplied by 0.02364658.
   - The number of special needs students is multiplied by 0.07666553.
8. Additional points are awarded based on the number of regular pupils of all schools in the community combined: 120 points if the number of

---

44 For details see Section 2, point 6 of http://data-onderwijs.vlaanderen.be/edulex/document.aspx?docid=14102.

students is between 900 and 3,999, 180 points if between 4,000 and 6,499. Then 60 additional points for each group of 1,500 additional students with a maximum of 420 points from 11,000 pupils.
9   120 points for part-time vocational education centers.

Global point envelope awarded to schools in full-time secondary education that do not belong to school communities
1   The same as for schools belonging to communities (see point *1)* above).
2   The same as for schools belonging to communities (see point 2) above).
3   Points used to hire the supporting staff point envelope
    –   The number of students entitled to additional teaching hours within GOK funding is multiplied by 0.2857.
    –   The number of other students (not entitled to GOK-funding) is multiplied by 0.2741.
    –   The weekly teaching hours for schools that are entitled to GOK funding are multiplied by 0.2651.
    –   The other school teaching hours are multiplied by 0.2544.
4   Points awarded for function and task differentiation.
    –   The number of regular students is multiplied by 0.02316074.
    –   The weekly package teaching hours is multiplied by 0.01970700.
5   120 points are for part-time vocational education centers (Vlaamse Overheid, 2009).

Operations budgets
The financing of operations for secondary schools is based on the same elements as for primary education – i.e. objective differences, student characteristics and school characteristics (Groenez, Juchtmans, Smet, & Stevens, 2015).

The calculation of funding based on objective differences (the first element) is the same as for primary education, so we will not describe it again.

Student characteristics
As for primary schools, the second element that decides the operations budget of secondary school boards is the student characteristics in these schools. The student characteristics are measured by the same 4 indicators (educational level of the mother, educational grant, mother tongue and neighborhood). For secondary schools, the percentage set aside to compensate for student characteristics increases on an annual base from 10.5625% in 2016 to 11% in 2019. This budget is for secondary education then equally distributed across the four indicators. The rest of the calculation copies the calculation for primary schools.

School characteristics

The third element that influences the operating funds is the so-called school characteristics. These school characteristics are the educational level, educational type and the students' area of study. In mainstream secondary education only level (cycle) and field of study are relevant. After setting aside money for the objective differences and the budget for student characteristics the remainder of the original budget for secondary education is distributed according to these school characteristics. Each of these characteristics has a weighting coefficient and a point value. For students in the first cycle and students in the second and third cycles of general secondary education, the point value is set at 16. For students in technical and vocational education in the second and third cycles, the point value of 18 or 22 is applied depending on the field of study. For students in the second or third cycle of ballet and podium arts the point value of 20 is used, and for visual arts students a weight of 18 is applied. Finally, nursing students receive a value of 20 points.

For instance, a school with 20 general secondary education students in the second cycle and 30 students doing ballet receives:

$$20 \times 16 + 30 \times 20 = 920 \, points.$$

The budget for school characteristics is then divided by the sum of the point values of all students. This quotient determines the amount a school receives per point.

Point envelope ICT

Another source of income is the financing of ICT operations. These are based on the weighted number of students (the weighting coefficients differ for different tracks) and multiplied by a budgetary coefficient of 0.7163.

Type of track	Coefficient
The reception class for non-dutch-speaking newcomers in secondary education, The B stream[45] of the first grade of full-time secondary education, The pupils of the second, third and fourth years of vocational secondary education, Nursing, Part-time vocational secondary education, Part-time secondary sea-fishing education and special secondary education.	1.25

---

45 The so-called B stream is intended for students who have not obtained a certificate of primary education, have a learning deficiency or are less suitable for predominantly theoretical education. After one year in the B stream, such students can transfer to the A stream.

Type of track	Coefficient
The A stream of the first grade of full-time secondary education, The second and third grades of general secondary education, art secondary education and technical secondary education	1

Thus, a school with 200 students in general secondary education and the A stream of the first grade of full-time secondary education would receive 200 × 1 × 0.7163 = 143.26 EUR. These resources can only be used for logistical and material support of ICT coordination.

Calculation of allocations

After computing the points for each and approving the final budget, the school boards receive allocations proportionally according to their points.

An example of a secondary school board budget in Flanders

In Flanders, the school board receives the funding and then distributes it to the schools it governs. Therefore, in this box, we present an example of the budget of a Flemish community school board in 2014/15 (the system of calculation has not changed). The example is based on Nusche et al. (2015). In this example, we take a secondary school with 296 students consisting of 46 2nd cycle ASO students, 43 3rd cycle ASO students, 36 2nd cycle TSO students, 36 3rd cycle TSO students, 69 2nd cycle BSO students, and 66 3rd cycle BSO students.

The total allocation is composed of staff and operating budget. We will not discuss the operating budget in detail as it is very similar to the one for primary schools.

Staff formation

The staff funding consists mostly of principal and teaching staff funding. Since the school has 296 students, it receives a fully funded principal without a teaching assignment.

The funding of teaching staff is determined as (see Appendices "The types of education classes")

1. 2nd cycle ASO 46 students: 83.2 hours
   a. According to scales 25 × 1.9 + 21 × 1.7 = 83.2
2. 3rd cycle ASO 43 students: 78.1 hours
   a. According to scales 25 × 1.9 + 18 × 1.7 = 78.1
3. 2nd cycle TSO 36 students: 15.8 + 78.9 = 94.7 hours (but the minimum package is 156 hours)

a. According to scales 25 × 0.5 + 11 × 0.3 = 15.8
    b. Teaching according to groups 11 × 2.05 + 12 × 2.15 + 13 × 2.35 = 78.9
4. 3rd cycle TSO 36 students: 15.8 + 78.9 = 94.8 hours (but the minimum package is 156 hours)
    a. According to scales 25 × 0.5 + 11 × 0.3 = 15.8
    b. Teaching according to groups 14 × 2.05 + 7 × 2.15 + 15 × 2.35 = 79
5. 2nd cycle BSO 69 students: 219.45 hours
    a. According to scales 25 × 0.6 + 44 × 0.3 = 28.2
    b. Teaching according to groups 17 × 2.45 + 18 × 2.55 + 34 × 3.05 = 191.25
6. 3rd cycle BSO 66 students: 201.9 hours
    a. According to scales 25 × 0.6 + 41 × 0.3 = 27.3
    b. Teaching according to groups 17 × 2.45 + 21 × 2.55 + 18 × 3.05 = 174.6

This gives a total of 894.65 hours (including minimum package)

Furthermore, the school board would receive some complementary teaching hours based on religion and non-confessional ethics. These are determined as follows (taken from Nusche et al., 2015).

Study year	Norm	RC	Prot	J	Isl	Ort	Ang	Ncz	Ecr	Cb	Total
Year 1, Stage 2, ASO	27	2	2	0	2	0	0	2	0	0	8
Year 2, Stage 2, ASO	27	2	0	0	2	0	0	2	0	0	6
Year 1, Stage 2, BSO	27	2	0	0	2	0	0	2	0	0	6
Year 2, Stage 2, BSO	27	2	0	0	0	0	0	2	0	0	4
Year 1, Stage 2, TSO	27	2	0	0	2	0	0	2	0	0	6
Year 2, Stage 2, TSO	27	2	0	0	2	0	0	2	0	0	6
Year 1, Stage 3, ASO	27	2	0	0	2	0	0	2	0	0	6
Year 2, Stage 3, ASO	27	2	0	0	2	0	0	2	0	0	6
Year 1, Stage 3, BSO	27	2	0	0	0	0	0	2	0	0	4
Year 2, Stage 3, BSO	27	2	0	0	2	0	0	2	0	0	6
Year 3, Stage 3, BSO	27	2	0	0	0	0	0	2	0	0	4
Year 1, Stage 3, TSO	27	2	0	0	0	0	0	2	0	0	4
Year 1, Stage 3, TSO	27	2	0	0	0	0	0	2	0	0	4
Total		26	2	0	16	0	0	26	0	0	70

Where RC: Roman Catholic; Pro: Protestant; J: Jewish; Isl: Islamic; Ort: Orthodox; Ang: Anglican; Ncz: Non-confessional ethics; Ecr: Éthique et culture réligieuse (non-recognised option); CB: Cultural awareness (non-recognised option). In total, the school will obtain 70 hours.

As mentioned above, the teaching hours obtained are multiplied by application rates and rounded:
- General teaching hours 582.65 × 0.9657 = 563 hours
- Minimum package hours 312 × 0.9857 = 308 hours
- Teaching hours for religion 70 × 0.98 = 69 hours

> Lastly, the school board would receive points for ICT (note that here the weighting coefficient differs). These points are given as
>
> $$(161 \text{ (A stream students)} \times 1 + 135 \text{ (B stream students)} \times 1.25 + 234 \text{ (part-time vocational)} \times 1.25) \times 0.03969 = 25 \text{ points}$$
>
> So in total, the school receives 871 teaching hours, 69 teaching hours for religion and non-confessional ethics and 25 points for ICT coordination.
>
> The school board receives funding for objective difference, student characteristics, school characteristics and point envelope for ICT.
>
> Since community schools are required to teach religiously neutral education, they are entitled to compensation for objective differences. The funding per students is, consequently, in the end increased by 4.5 percent. In our case, this would be approximately $(116{,}234.22 + 3{,}694.1 + 161.17) \times 0.045 = 5{,}404.02$ EUR.
>
> Further, as an operating budget, the school board receives funding for objective difference, student characteristics, school characteristics and point envelope for ICT. The calculation has the same structure as for primary schools.

Special needs education

The only difference between primary mainstream and special needs education is in the funding based on school characteristics, which is one of the elements of the operations budget. As mentioned above for mainstream primary education, the point value per student is set at 8.[46] For special needs students integrated in primary schools, we summarize the additional points that schools get in Table 13.

Type	Additional Points
Integrated education – Partial and permanent integration	1.1
Integrated education – Full and permanent integration of normally gifted students with a certificate of special education type 3 or 9	4.4
Integrated education – Full and permanent integration of normally gifted students with a certificate of special education type 4 or 7	5.5

Table 13: Additional points for specials students integrated in mainstream education; source: Vlaamse Overheid (1998).

---

46 For nursery schools (2.5 to 6 years), the point value is 6.

Special needs students' funding
In Flanders, there are two systems of schooling for special needs students – students within mainstream education and students in special schools. These two groups are also funded separately.

The first group of schools receive funding based on the rules described above. And since school characteristics (including a share of special needs students) is one of the determinants of schools' funding, special needs hours within mainstream education are allocated to pupils who need extra support because they have fallen behind in development or learning. There is also a small group of about 100 special needs students enrolled in mainstream schools within the inclusive education project (ION). Those are children with a moderate or severe intellectual disability who receive supplementary teaching periods and also an integration allowance (European Commission/EACEA/Eurydice, 2017). According to the European Agency for Special Needs and Inclusive Education (2017), however, the funding for special needs students in mainstream education in only a fraction of that for those in special schools, which creates a financial barrier to the integration of such students. This situation should improve with the new rules coming in in the 2017/2018 academic year.

From that year on, mainstream schools receive support in working with students with special educational needs from the special needs schools. The support will be provided from a support network where schools for ordinary and extraordinary education will combine the expertise of teachers from both types of schools. This support network will replace the GON and ION integration programs.

According to the new rules, there will be two models of support in primary and secondary education. First is support for mainstream schools with students classified as having type 2 (moderate to severe mental handicap), type 4 (physical handicap), type 6 (visual handicap) or type 7 (auditory handicap). Such mainstream schools with special needs students will be provided with support from special schools of relevant types. The special schools that have already established such networks will continue to cooperate. Second, it is the model of support for mainstream schools with students classified as having type 3 (emotional or behavioral disorder), type 7 (speech or language handicap) and type 9 (severe learning disabilities).[47] Networks of special schools to support student with these types of disabilities will be formed and they will be focused on mild mental handicaps or autism without mental handicap (types 1 and 8), speech or language disorder (3 and 7) and severe learning difficulties (9).

---

47 http://data-onderwijs.vlaanderen.be/edulex/document.aspx?docid=15071#2, accessed July 29, 2017.

The funding for cooperation within the first model is generated by students with disability type 2, 4, 6 or 7 as defined in the Basic Education Act or the Secondary Education Code, and students with the same type of disability who fall under the transitional measure in the M decree (former GON students). In 2017/2018, special schools will receive in total 14,567.5 guidance units (teaching or other hours). In 2018/2019, a package of 14,804 units will be adjusted with the evolution of the number of such special needs students in mainstream education schools. One of the distinct features of the new system is that the government will no longer determine a number of hours of guidance per week per student according to the type of disability. This will be done by the schools and teachers on their own. The allocated guidance units can be transformed into extra hours, extra classes and schools can set up the position of teaching staff or paramedical, medical, social, psychological and orthopedagogical staff (including for instance speech therapists, physiotherapists, occupational therapists, child welfare officers, nurses, medical doctors, social workers etc.).

Regarding the funding of cooperation within the second model, there is a transition period of three academic years (from 2017/2018 to 2019/2020) in order to adjust to the new system from GON and ION. Starting from 2020/2021, the allocation will be calculated based on the number of pupils in mainstream schools in a support network (with a weight of 70 percent in the calculation) and on the average number of students with special needs during the last 6 school years in the mainstream schools within a network (with a weight of 30 percent). Currently until 2019-2020, no permanent staff can be hired within this system.

As can be seen, this system will distribute a total allocation which is set in advance rather than compute per student numbers at first and then calculate the total allocation based on the number of students.

Network of special schools

A large proportion of special needs students are still enrolled in separate special needs schools. Since the funding of special education in special schools follows different rules, we will discuss the funding of such schools separately. The allocation, like that for mainstream schools, consists of funding for staff and operation budgets. The funding for staff covers the principal's salary, teaching staff, paramedic, medical, social, psychological and orthopedagogical staff, points and replacement. In this book, we will discuss mostly the funding for staff as it is the main difference from the mainstream schools' funding.

Principal's salary
In each special school, a principal is funded or partially funded. In small special schools, a principal is required to teach 14 lessons if they have fewer than 20 students and 8 lessons if they have 20 to 39 students. Otherwise, a school principal's full-time position is funded. In the case of a merger a deputy director can also be funded (Vlaamse Overheid, 2005).

Teaching staff
Teaching staff are funded based on the number of hours needed in a school. There are three types of lessons: (i) teaching time according to the scale; (ii) additional lessons (for neutrality and religion, permanent education at home, integrated education (GON), the inclusive education project (ION), for the integration of Dutch non-native speakers, for the provision of an equal education opportunity policy etc.; and (iii) additional teaching times (in the case of a voluntary merger, temporary home education or in the event of aberrations).

Teaching time according to the scale is based on the number of students enrolled. The allocations per student differ with respect to the type of special education a student attends.[48] For instance, a school with 10 students would get 32 teaching hours if the students' special needs were of type 1 and 8, 47 hours if they were of types 2, 3, 4, 5 and 9, and 56 for those of types 6 and 7. The number of teaching hours is added up across types and multiplied by a rate of 0.945, then the number is reduced by possible hours of instruction by a school principal and a deputy principal. The remaining hours are allocated to the teaching staff. In order to get the number of full-time teachers to be hired, the remaining hours are divided by the number of hours that a teacher can teach per week (usually 24). Furthermore, some share of the teaching hours according to the scale is used for the most frequent religion in a school, non-confessional doctrine or culture.

Additional lessons are allocated in order to provide extra lessons for courses in other (less often practiced) recognized religions or non-confessional doctrine, lessons for permanent education at home, and extra lessons for the integration of non-native speakers in the Dutch language. The additional lessons in Dutch are targeted at primary schools located on the linguistic borders and the borders with the municipalities of the Brussels-Capital Region. Schools with fewer than 10 percent of students in primary and lower secondary education are not entitled to the additional

---

48 The full tables can be downloaded from http://data-onderwijs.vlaanderen.be/edulex/bestand.ashx?nr=1918 [accessed on 04/09/2017].

lessons. Schools with 10 to 25 percent of primary and lower secondary students get 6 additional lessons. Those with 25 to 40 percent receive 6 additional lessons plus + 0.315 × number of students above 25 percent of the total student number. Schools with 40 percent or more of primary and lower secondary students get 6 additional lessons + 0.4 × number of students above 25 percent of the total student number. The additional lessons awarded are used to establish positions of teachers or special physical education teachers. Additional lessons may also be awarded to a principal or a deputy director.

The allocations per student differ with respect to the type of special education (one of the nine groups) they attend. Each of the nine types of special education at the level of basic education has its own coefficient. The coefficient is most favorable for children with types 6 and 7 – a visual or auditory disability. As of the 2009/2010 school year, special schools offering education types 1 and/or 3 receive additional resources (teaching hours, guidance and support), depending on the number of pupils who meet the equal educational opportunities indicator of 'mother's level of education'.

Additional teaching times are provided in a voluntary merger of two schools. One of those schools is allowed to receive the difference between the funding that would be allocated to the separate schools minus the funding that a merged school would receive in the first year. This additional teaching gradually decreases over time to 0 after 4 years from the merger.

Paramedic, medical, social, psychological and orthopedagogical staff
As in the case of teaching staff, the number of funded posts is determined by the number of hours assumed to be needed for students of a school. There are three types of these hours: (i) hours according to the target numbers; (ii) additional hours for integrated students (such as GON, ION; will in the future be replaced by a different system, see above); and (iii) additional hours in the event of aberrations.

Hours according to the target numbers are calculated as the sum of the product: students per type × target number. Target numbers per type are summarized in Table 14. The funds from this allocation can be used to hire psychologists, doctors, nurses, speech therapists, physiotherapists, social workers etc. The number of full-time posts should be taken from the hours worked per week. This is assumed to be 40 for a doctor, psychologist or orthopedagogist: 32 for a physiotherapist, occupational therapist, childcare worker, nurse and social worker and 30 for a speech therapist.

Type of education	Target number
Type of basic offer	1
Type 1	1
Type 2	3.9
Type 3	2.1
Type 4	5
Type 6	2.1
Type 7	2.9
Type 8	1
Type 9	2.1

Table 14: Target numbers for different types of disabilities; source: Vlaamse Overheid (2005).

Regarding additional hours in the event of aberrations, the Flemish government might grant additional reading hours for teaching staff and/or additional hours for paramedical, medical, social, psychological and orthopedagogical staff at the request of a school board of a primary education school due to special circumstances. These additional hours cannot be used for hiring new permanent employees.

Point envelopes
As in primary and secondary education, schools receive certain point envelopes used to calculate funding for care coordinators, ICT coordinators, and administrative employees. These are computed per student and they generally do not differ for different types of disability.

For instance, each school receives a minimum of 9 points for administrative employees. In addition, each school is entitled to a number of additional points. Schools also receive ICT point calculated as the number of students × 1.25 × 0.03969.

Replacement units are additional teaching hours that can be used only to cover short absences of employees for which there are no alternative compensation measures. They are calculated similarly as in mainstream education.

Operations budgets
School boards are entitled to operations budgets for the operation, equipment and major maintenance of their schools, for working on the rational use of energy in their schools and to provide free equipment mentioned in Article 27 of the Primary Education Act (which includes textbooks, scripts, workbooks and magazines, photocopies, software, ICT material etc.) (Vlaamse Overheid, 1997).

As for mainstream education, for the purposes of calculating operations budgets, student characteristics and school characteristics apply. Student characteristics are determined by mother's level of education, whether a student obtains a school allowance, whether the language the student speaks in the family differs from the language of instruction, and whether a pupil has his place of residence in a neighborhood with a high percentage of students at least two years behind in schooling at the age of 15.

There are 7 types of school characteristics with respect to what type of education they provide. These types are school boards organizing pre-primary education (type 1), school boards organizing primary education (type 2), school boards organizing special kindergartens with the exception of type 4 special education (type 3), school boards organizing special kindergartens of type 4 (type 4), school boards organizing special lower education with the exception of type 4 special education (type 5), school boards organizing primary special education of type 4 (type 6), school boards of primary education supervising one or more pupils in integrated primary education (type 7).

The operations budget per school is then calculated using a per capita formula partly based on school characteristics and student characteristics.

An example of the budget of a school with special needs students in Flanders

In Flanders, the school board receives the funding, and then distributes it to the schools it governs. Therefore, in this box we present an example of the budget of a Flemish provincial school board (OGO). The calculation follows the funding formula described above. We take a primary school with 180 students, of whom 10 are special needs students with a certificate of special education type 9 (severe learning disabilities). To make the example more interesting, we assume that 20 students come from non-Dutch-speaking families, 10 receive educational grants and 5 come from the traveling population (such as the Roma people).

The total allocation is composed of staff and operating budget.

Staff formation
The staff funding consists of principal funding, teaching staff and point envelopes. Since the school has 180 students, it receives a fully funded principal without a teaching assignment.

The funding of teaching staff is determined as $175 \times 1 + 5 \times 1.5 = 182.5$ weighted students. The 5 students are the Roma students that are weighted by 1.5. According to the table from Appendix 2 of the Basic Education Law (http://data-onderwijs.vlaanderen.be/documenten/bestand.ashx?nr=5100), this weighted number of students generates 236 teaching hours. And then a coefficient of 0.9716 is applied, yielding the final number of teaching hours, 229. By dividing this by the number of teaching hours per teacher (24), we receive 9.5 full-time equivalent positions.

Furthermore, the school board would receive some complementary teaching hours based on the religion of its students. This is determined by paragraph 3.2.1.3 of the circular on Staff Formation in Mainstream Primary Schools (http://data-onderwijs.vlaanderen.be/edulex/document.aspx?docid=13615#3-2-1-3). Assuming that the majority of students would opt for non-confessional ethics (about 100 students), 60 for Christianity and 20 Muslim, the school board would get 12 complementary hours and approximately 4 and 2 complementary hours for Christian and Muslim teaching.

Lastly, the school board would receive $180 \times 1.25 \times 0.03969 = 8.93$ points for ICT and $180 \times 01543 = 27.77$ points for administration. The exact specification of who can be hired based on these points is given in the same circular paragraph 1.4.1.3 (see http://data-onderwijs.vlaanderen.be/edulex/document.aspx?docid=13641#1-4-1-3).

Operating budget
The school board receives funding for objective difference, student characteristics, school characteristics and point envelope for ICT.

Since community schools are required to teach religiously neutral education, they are entitled to compensation for objective differences. The funding per students is, consequently, in the end increased by 4.5 percent. In our case, this would be $(116{,}234.22 + 3{,}694.1 + 161.17) \times 0.045 = 5{,}404.02$ EUR.

The additional funding based on student characteristics is calculated as 15 percent of the total budget for primary schools, divided by 4 and then distributed equally among the 4 categories (low educational level of the mother, receiver of a school grant, non-Dutch home language and living in a poor neighborhood). In 2017, the funding per non-Dutch home language was 128.66 EUR and the funding per student receiving educational grants was 112.09 EUR. So it is $128.66 \times 20 = 2{,}573.20$ EUR for non-Dutch home language students and $112.09 \times 10 = 1{,}120.90$ EUR for students receiving educational grants. In total, the student characteristics funding was 3,694.1 EUR.

Since we assume a primary school board, the points for school characteristics are computed as follows 170 × 8 + 10 × (8 + 4.4) = 1,484 points, where 4.4 is additional funding per special needs student with a certificate of type 9 (see ; this is the only part of the funding system for mainstream schools which differs for special needs students integrated in such schools). In 2017, one point was equivalent to 80.72 EUR, thus the total funding for our school board would be 119,788.48 EUR (equivalent of 665.50 EUR per student for this particular school board).

For 10 special needs schools, the school board receives additional funding for staff formation (for details, see https://pincette.vsko.be/meta/properties/dc-identifier/Bes-20161116-1). The per student supplement for such special needs students was in 2016/2017 set to 248.43 EUR so the school board would receive additional funding of 2,484.30 EUR.

And, lastly, the school board receives funds for ICT operating budgets. These are calculated as 180 × 1.25 × 0.7163 = 161.17 EUR and can only be used for logistic and material support of the ICT coordination.

Area	Allocations in points of EUR
Staff information	
– School principal	1 position without teaching obligations
– Teaching staff	9.5 full-time eq. positions
– Complementary teaching hours	18 teaching hours
– Point envelope	8.93 points for ICT + 27.77 points for administration
Operating budgets	129 207.72 EUR
– School characteristics	119,788.48 EUR
– Objective differences	Additional 4.5 % of total funding 5,563.97 EUR
– Student characteristics	3,694.1 EUR
– ICT operating budget	161.17 EUR

Table 15: Allocations to a Flemish community school board; source: Authors.

The funding for this model school board is summarized in Table 15. For staff formation, it would receive funding for a principal, 9.5 full-time equivalent positions for teaching staff, 18 teaching hours for teaching religion, 8.93 points for ICT and 27.77 points for administration. The funding from the points (such as for school characteristics) is calculated proportionally according to the points that school boards receive from the overall remaining budget for all school boards (i.e. if there were 2 school boards with 100 and 200 points, respectively, the first would receive 1/3 of the remaining budget and the second 2/3). For operating budgets, it

> would receive 129,207.72 EUR which mostly comes from the funding for school characteristics.
>
> The school boards then usually simply split the total budget (after putting some part aside as a reserve) according to the number of students in each school (if a school board manages more than one school).

Summary of the Flemish education funding system

The education funding system in Flanders is more rigorous compared to the other regions and countries in this study and is determined mostly based on per student funding. It also takes into account the socio-economic status of students and allocates funds that are directed to various types of spending such as ICT, but cannot be spent otherwise.

The funds are allocated to school boards and not to strictly demographically determined districts or municipalities. Furthermore, the school boards do not enjoy that much flexibility in choosing how they spend the allocated funds, which is also in contrast to the practice in the other regions and countries studied, where school districts or municipalities receive lump-sum allocation and they choose on their own what to do with it.

Regarding the funding of special schools, there are two distinct systems. Mainstream schools receive additional funding as part of the operations budgets where special needs students co-determine school characteristics that are used to calculate the allocations. The number of integrated students in mainstream education is limited and the lowest among the EU countries; however, the system will change and the number of integrated students should increase as there will be provided and funded special support from so-called support networks for special needs students within mainstream schools.

Separate special schools are funded differently. They receive funding for the teaching time based on the number of students enrolled and with respect to the 9 types of special education. Moreover, they are entitled to special funding for paramedic, medical, social, psychological and orthopedagogical staff which is also mainly determined by the number of students and differs for different types of special needs education.

Below, we summarize some strengths and weaknesses of the Flemish funding formula. Furthermore, Figure 8 presents the main components of total allocation to Flemish school boards.

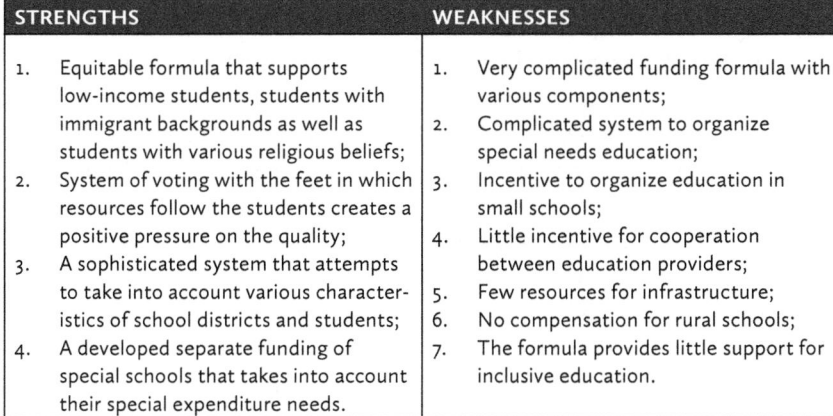

STRENGTHS	WEAKNESSES
1. Equitable formula that supports low-income students, students with immigrant backgrounds as well as students with various religious beliefs;	1. Very complicated funding formula with various components;
2. System of voting with the feet in which resources follow the students creates a positive pressure on the quality;	2. Complicated system to organize special needs education;
	3. Incentive to organize education in small schools;
3. A sophisticated system that attempts to take into account various characteristics of school districts and students;	4. Little incentive for cooperation between education providers;
	5. Few resources for infrastructure;
	6. No compensation for rural schools;
4. A developed separate funding of special schools that takes into account their special expenditure needs.	7. The formula provides little support for inclusive education.

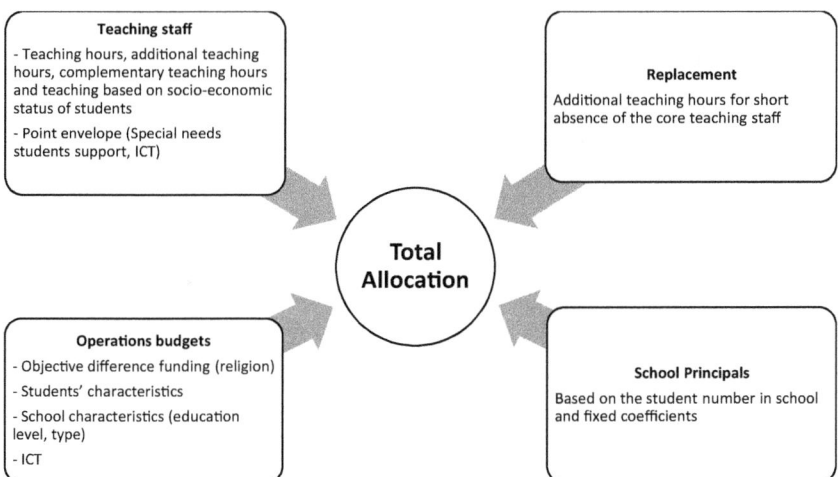

Figure 8: Simplified diagram of the main components of total allocation to primary school boards in Flanders; source: Authors.

4.5 Massachusetts

The Massachusetts funding formula covers K12 education so it is the same for primary, secondary and special education.[49] The formula uses so-called

---

49 In this overview, we do not cover federal funding which constitutes about 5% of the total funding for schools in Massachusetts (MassBudget.org, 2010). The federal funding comes from two sources: Title I (as part of formerly No Child Left Behind and now Every Student Succeeds) and IDEA (Innovative Diversity Efforts Awards) project-based grants.

enrolment foundation which is a count of the number of students for whom a school district is responsible (including students from other districts that attend education in the school district). The enrollment foundation is then multiplied by different cost rates assigned according to 12 discrete categories (Massachusetts Department of Elementary and Secondary Education, 2017a):
- regular education pre-kindergarten
- special education pre-kindergarten
- regular or special education half-day kindergarten
- regular or special education full-day kindergarten
- regular or special education elementary (grades 1-5)
- regular or special education junior high/middle (grades 6-8)
- regular or special education senior high (grades 9-13)
- limited English pre-kindergarten
- limited English half-day kindergarten
- limited English (grades 1-12)
- vocational education (grades 9-12)
- post-secondary and post-graduate vocational education (grade 13)

These categories are determined as types of education and the time/resources requirements of the students in those types, and they cover all primary, secondary and special needs education. Still, for the sake of consistency, we split the actual calculation of the part on primary and secondary education. Before we do so let us describe the general mechanisms behind the formula.

The mechanism behind the formula

Unlike the other funding formulas analyzed in this book, Massachusetts, instead of weighting an overall foundation amount based on the number of students in particular categories, uses a formula that weights the costs of individual resources.[50]

Therefore, the per pupil costs associated with teachers, benefits, materials, professional development, etc. (known as "functions") are not constant from student to student. Instead, each input has a different cost for every category of students. Districts are funded for the line-item costs associated with the make-up of their particular student bodies. Above and beyond these allocations, districts also receive flat amounts (rather than weighted

---

50 The formula used in Massachusetts is in this aspect also different from those used in different US states.

amounts) for students in other categories, such as low-income students (called the local contribution which is computed from the wealth and income taxes) and students in certain types of special education placements.

Massachusetts incorporates the funding of special needs education into its general equalization funding formula (known as "Chapter 70 Aid"), and by assigning greater values to those "functions" (teachers, materials etc.) in which students with disabilities need additional resources. The state uses a census model that assumes constant numbers of students with disabilities rather than counting actual enrolments of students with special needs. Notably, special education is the only part of the formula that uses this census model. Massachusetts also uses an excess cost grant to reimburse districts' catastrophic special education expenditures (Connecticut School of Finance, 2016).

The calculation of allocations

The Massachusetts funding allocation to primary and secondary schools can be calculated in three steps that are as follows:
1. Calculation of foundation budget
2. Calculation of required local contribution
3. Filling the gap with Chapter 70 education aid

We describe these steps in detail below. It should be noted that this is a minimum that municipalities have to contribute to their primary school districts.[51] A municipality can, similarly as in e.g. Finland, decide to contribute more to the school districts.

Foundation budget calculation for primary schools
In the following text, we distinguish between elementary and junior high/middle students. Both groups attend primary education; however, the funding differs. The Massachusetts funding formula for primary schools uses so-called foundation enrolment which is a count of the number of primary education students for whom a school district is responsible on October 1 (including students from other districts that attend primary schools[52] in Massachusetts).

In order to calculate the foundation budget, the enrolment foundation is multiplied by different cost rates assigned according to 12 discrete categories

---

51 In reality, this calculation also includes secondary schools. However, since the main aim is to describe primary education funding, we omit secondary schools even though the mechanisms are very similar.
52 We consider elementary and junior high/middle schools as primary education (grades 1-8).

(9 base components and 3 incremental costs above the base categories for special education and economically disadvantaged students; Massachusetts Department of Elementary and Secondary Education, 2017a). The categories most relevant for primary education are:
- regular or special education elementary (grades 1-5)
- regular or special education junior high/middle (grades 6-8)

The categories are determined as types of education and time/resources requirements of the students in those types. Unlike the other funding formulas in this study, Massachusetts, instead of weighting an overall foundation amount based on the number of students in particular categories, uses a formula that weights the costs of individual resources.[53]

Therefore, the per pupil costs associated with teachers, benefits, materials, professional development, etc. (known as "functions") are not constant from student to student. Instead, each input has a different cost for every category of primary education student. Districts are funded for the line-item costs associated with the make-up of their particular student bodies.

In Table 16, we summarize these cost rates relevant for primary education in Massachusetts in 2017/18. The coefficient of 81.7 percent of the state-wide average expenditure – that is repeatedly used in the calculation of the cost rates – was chosen since this factor generated the same state-wide funding as would have been generated by the old formula.

	Elementary	Junior high/middle
Administration	81.7 percent of 2003/04 state average expenditure per pupil for administration, factored up by inflation.	
	$498	
Instructional Leadership	81.7 percent of FY04 state average expenditure per pupil for instructional leadership, factored up by inflation.	
	$680	
Classroom And Specialist Teachers	Based on average salary of $38,000 in 2003/04, factored up by inflation to $67,885 per teacher, and assumed class sizes of 22 for elementary, 25 for junior high/middle.	
	$3,048	$2,682

---

53   The formula used in Massachusetts is in this aspect also different from those used in different US states.

FUNDING FORMULAS

	Elementary	Junior high/middle
Other Teaching Services	81.7 percent of the FY04 state average expenditure per pupil for other teaching services, factored up by inflation. Adjusted by the coefficients 1.25 for elementary and 0.9 for junior high/middle.	
	$781	$563
Professional Development	3 percent of the salary of teachers and support staff, factored up by inflation.	
	$121	$131
Instructional Equipment And Technology	Statutory per pupil amounts factored up by inflation.	
	$441	
Guidance And Psychological	81.7 percent of FY04 state average expenditure per pupil for guidance and psychological, factored up by inflation and adjusted by the coefficients 0.75 for elementary and 1.0 for junior high/middle.	
	$222	$295
Pupil Services	Combined statutory per pupil rates: $50 for health staff, $50 for athletics, and $25 other activities at elementary and $35 at junior high/middle.	
	$132	$216
Operations And Maintenance	Combined statutory assumptions for custodial salaries (0.1 × the number of foundation teaching and support staff, at a salary of $25,000); maintenance ($3,300 × the number of foundation teaching and support staff); and extraordinary maintenance ($2,200 × the number of foundation teaching and support staff), factored up by inflation.	
	$846	$918
Special Education Tuition	Statutory assumption for special education tuition rate of $13,500 per pupil, factored up by inflation	
	$23,853	

Table 16: Costs rates for primary education in Massachusetts, amounts are per pupil in 2017/18; source: http://www.doe.mass.edu/finance/chapter70/chapter-cal-rates.xlsx.

An example of a primary school district budget in Massachusetts

In this box, we present an example of the budget of a school district in Massachusetts. The presented budget follows the real budgets published on the website of the Massachusetts Department of Elementary and Secondary Education (http://www.doe.mass.edu/finance/statistics/ppx12-16.html). In this example, we take the district of North Brookfield that runs one primary and one secondary school.

There were 682.1 full-time equivalent students enrolled in this district in 2016/2017.

The districts receive money in 10 areas, as seen in Table 17. In Column 2, we show the per student allocation in the respective areas. The sum of all areas is 13,492.73 EUR which is the average per student allocation that the district received in 2016/2017. The total funding is then simply given as the per student amount multiplied by the number of students (682.1). This yields the total allocation of $ 9,203,391.13.

Area	Amount per student in U.S. dollars
Administration	738.39
Instructional leadership	823.83
Teachers	4,779.62
Other teaching services	929.65
Professional development	160,11
Instructional materials, equipment and technology	606,51
Guidance counseling and testing	411,32
Pupil services	1 407,28
Operations and maintenance	1 232,11
Insurance, retirement programs and others	2,782.90
Total	13,492.73
Total per district	9,203,391.13

Table 17: Overview of pupil expenditures by major functional categories in North Brookfield; source: Massachusetts Department of Elementary and Secondary Education (2016).

The district can then decide on the exact funding for each school. A simple version is that it redistributes the allocation into two schools on a per student basis with regard to the cost rates as it was calculated on the state level.

Above and beyond these allocations, primary education districts also receive flat amounts (rather than weighted amounts) for students in other categories, such as low-income students (called the local contribution which is computed from the wealth and income taxes) and students in certain types of special education placements (for details see the sub-chapter on special needs education below). Low-income students are identified based on participation in state-administered programs such as the Supplemental Nutrition Assistance Program (SNAP); Transitional Assistance for Families with Dependent Children (TAFDC); Department of Children and Families' (DCF) foster care program; or MassHealth (Medicaid) up to 133% of the federal poverty level (FPL). For instance, the district of Marshfield received approximately $4,000 per low-income pupil in 2017/18 (this calculation is also done using the abovementioned cost rates and differs district by district).

Foundation budget calculation for secondary schools
The Massachusetts funding formula for secondary schools uses so-called foundation enrolment which is a count of the number of secondary education students for whom a school district is responsible on October 1 (including students from other districts that attend secondary schools in Massachusetts). The mechanism is identical to the one used for primary schools; the difference is in the cost rates that are used in the calculation.

Thus to calculate the foundation budget the enrolment foundation is multiplied by different cost rates assigned according to 13 discrete categories (10 base components and 3 incremental costs above the base categories for special education and economically disadvantaged students; Massachusetts Department of Elementary and Secondary Education, 2017a). The categories most relevant for secondary education are:
- regular or special education senior high (grades 9-13)[54]
- vocational education (grades 9-12)

In Table 18, we summarize these cost rates relevant for secondary education in Massachusetts from 2017/18. The coefficient of 81.7 percent of the statewide average expenditure – that is repeatedly used in the calculation of the cost rates – was chosen since this factor generated the same statewide funding as would have been generated by the old formula.

---

54 Students in special education for life-skills and similar programs beyond the compulsory K12 curriculum in Massachusetts are considered to be students in grade 13.

	Secondary schools
Administration	81.7 percent of 2003/04 state average expenditure per pupil for administration, factored up by inflation.
	$498
Instructional leadership	81.7 percent of FY04 state average expenditure per pupil for instructional leadership, factored up by inflation.
	$680
Classroom and specialist teachers	Based on average salary of $38,000 in 2003/04, factored up by inflation to $67,885 per teacher, and assumed class sizes of 17 students.
	$3,944
Other teaching services	81.7 percent of the FY04 state average expenditure per pupil for other teaching services, factored up by inflation. Adjusted by the coefficient 0.75 for secondary schools.
	$468
Professional development	3 percent of the salary of teachers and support staff, factored up by inflation.
	$127
Instructional equipment and technology	Statutory per pupil amounts factored up by inflation.
	$706
Guidance and psychological	81.7 percent of FY04 state average expenditure per pupil for guidance and psychological help, factored up by inflation and adjusted by the coefficient 1.25 for secondary schools.
	$370
Pupil services	Combined statutory per pupil rates: $38 for health staff, $200 for athletics, and $45 other activities.
	$499
Operations and maintenance	Combined statutory assumptions for custodial salaries (0.1 × the number of foundation teaching and support staff, at a salary of $25,000); maintenance ($3,300 × the number of foundation teaching and support staff); and extraordinary maintenance ($2,200 × the number of foundation teaching and support staff), factored up by inflation.
	$890
Employee benefits and fixed charges	Combined statutory assumption for salary benefits ($4,320 × the number of foundation or all staff, adjusted by the wage adjustment factor + $468 × the same number of staff, not adjusted by the wage adjustment factor), factored up by inflation. An additional amount was added in 2017/18 in order to provide funding for the implementation of the 2015 recommendations of the Foundation Budget Review Commission.
	$796
Special education tuition	Statutory assumption for special education tuition rate of $13,500 per pupil, factored up by inflation
	$23,853

Table 18: Costs rates for secondary education in Massachusetts, amounts are per pupil in 2017/18; source: http://www.doe.mass.edu/finance/chapter70/chapter-cal-rates.xlsx.

As well as primary school districts, secondary school districts also receive flat amounts (rather than weighted amounts) for students in other categories, such as low-income students (called the local contribution which is computed from the wealth and income taxes) and students in certain types of special education placements (for details see the sub-chapter on special needs education below). For instance, the district of Marshfield received approximately $4,000 per low-income pupil in 2017/18 (this calculation is also done using the abovementioned cost rates and differs district by district).

Wage Factor
As in British Columbia, there is also a wage adjustment factor put in place in Massachusetts. The mechanism is the same for primary and secondary schools. The rationale behind this factor is that it is more costly to attract school teachers and other staff in areas with higher average salaries. There were 23 labor market areas established in Massachusetts. The latest available average wage data (including all industries, both private and public) from the state's Department of Employment are used to calculate the city's and labor market area's wage factor[55] in each of these areas.

A weighted average of the labor market area's wage factor (80 percent) and the city's factor (20 percent) is used to determine a district's wage factor. The weighted wage factor is then divided by three to obtain the wage adjustment factor. This district-specific wage adjustment factor is then applied to the eight salary-related functional categories in the foundation budget – i.e. the funding for the salary-related cost categories differs across districts.

Since 2004, only those districts with above-average wages have been affected – i.e. districts' budgets are not reduced in low to average income areas. In 2017/18, only 110 cities in 3 labor market areas were affected.

Inflation
Foundation budget rates are adjusted each year by a statutorily defined inflationary factor. It affects all districts in the same way. The inflationary factor is calculated as the ratio of the current year's third-quarter inflation index to the prior year's third-quarter index.

---

55 By wage factor we simply mean the share of the average and the area's or city's average.

Required local contribution calculation

After the foundation budget is established, it is estimated how much a municipality in which the school district is located can contribute from local revenues to the schools. This is done by assuming uniform contributions by municipalities equal to

$$0.003 \times \text{municipality's total property values} + 0.014 \times \text{income earned by residents of the municipality}$$

Thus, the required local contribution is basically determined by the local tax revenue, assuming a constant willingness to fund the operation of its schools across municipalities.

Filling the gap with Chapter 70 education aid

The transfers under Chapter 70 from the state to municipalities that co-fund the school districts are then given as the difference between the foundation budget and the required local contribution which ensures that every district can produce funds at least at the level given by the foundation budget.

It should be noted that municipalities can add more funds than the foundation budget. These extra local contributions differ significantly across cities. In Figure 9, we show a comparison of two sample districts and their extra local contributions (MassBudget.org, 2010). In this example, you can see that despite a higher foundation budget in the district of Lynn (which is mostly the consequence of a large share of low-income and limited English students), the final per student contribution is higher in Newton. Newton decided to transfer higher extra local contributions to schools and, thus, the total actual budget is much higher.

An example of a secondary school district budget in Massachusetts

In this box, we present an example of the budget of a school district in Massachusetts. The presented budget follows the real budgets published on the website of the Massachusetts Department of Elementary and Secondary Education (http://www.doe.mass.edu/finance/statistics/ppx12-16.html). In this example, we take the district of North Brookfield that runs one primary and one secondary school. So this calculation shows funding for both primary and secondary schools as they are both part of the K-12 framework.

> There were 682.1 full-time equivalent students enrolled in this district in 2016/2017.
>
> The districts receive money in 10 areas, as seen in Table 17. In Column 2, we show the per student allocation in the respective areas. The sum of all areas is 13,492.73 EUR which is the average per student allocation that the district received in 2016/2017. The total funding is then simply given as the per student amount multiplied by the number of students (682.1). This yields the total allocation of $ 9,203,391.13.
>
> The district can then decide on the exact funding for each school. A simple version is that it redistributes the allocation into two schools on a per student basis with regard to the cost rates as calculated on the state level.

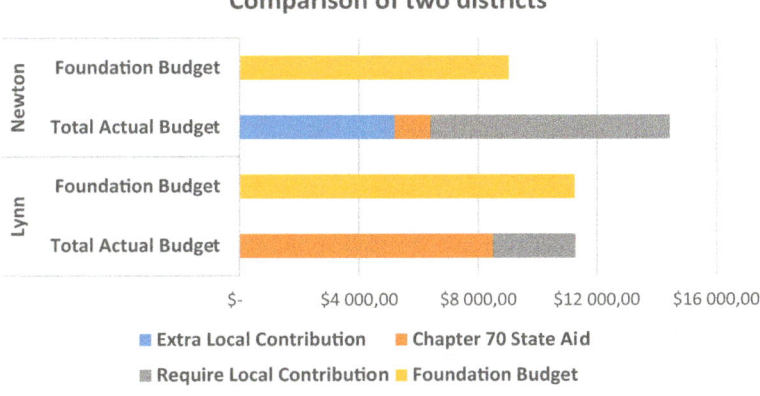

Figure 9: Comparison of schools per pupil spending in 2010 in two sample districts, source: MassBudget.org (2010).

Effective funding per student

By applying the above-described methodology for special education, the effective funding per full-time student equivalent in 2016 is as follows (Connecticut School of Finance, 2016):

In-District Placement (assumed 3.75 percent of non-vocational, 4.75 percent of vocational): 25,332 USD

Out-of-District Placement (assumed one percent of foundation enrollment): 26,461 USD

These numbers are higher than in other U.S. states, but it is necessary to keep in mind that it assumes a relatively low percentage of students with special needs and the amount is calculated per full-time equivalent student, not an individual student level. Figure 10 shows a comparison of budget rates per different student types included in the Chapter 70 Aid formula.

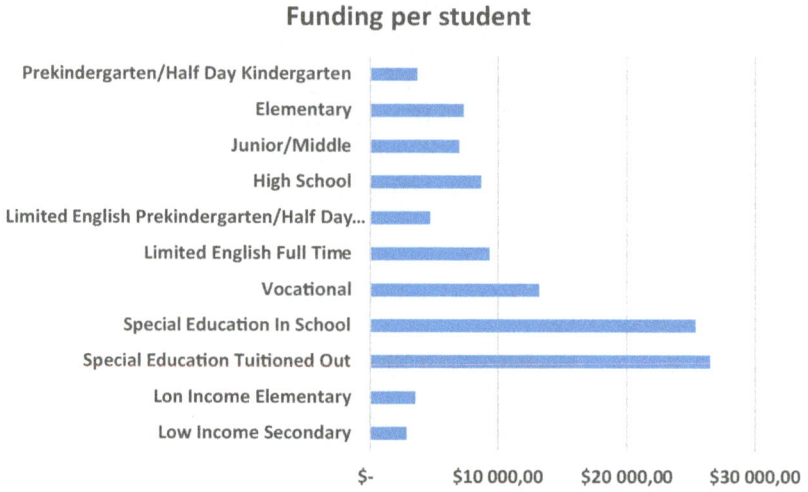

Figure 10: Comparison of Massachusetts' foundation budgets rates in 2016; source: Connecticut School of Finance (2016).

Funding outside the main formula

Apart from the funding determined by the Chapter 70 Aid, the state also funds a portion of the spending on "high-needs" special education students. The program for these students is called the Special Education Circuit Breaker and it started in 2004. It reimburses a portion of local spending on special needs students above a threshold. The formula for this kind of allocation changes every year depending on the state's funds that are available and the claim level. The threshold is given as four times the average foundation budget per pupil as calculated by the Chapter 70 Aid. The state is expected to pay 75 percent of the spending above this threshold, subject to the available funds. Between 2011 and 2014, the reimbursement rate averaged 73 percent.

In addition to the program, there is also the "extraordinary relief program" (funded up to 5 million USD) that was created to assist school districts with a significant increase in spending on special needs education. The criterion for eligibility is that a district experienced a 25 percent or greater increase in special education spending in the prior funding year.

Summary of the education funding in Massachusetts

The funding formula in the state of Massachusetts uses the so-called enrolment foundation which is a count of the number of students for whom a school district is responsible. The enrolment foundation is then multiplied by different cost rates (i.e. different cost rates for different components such as administration or classroom teachers, and also for different categories/types such as regular elementary education or regular junior high education). Figure 11 shows the main components that are taken into account in calculating these cost rates.

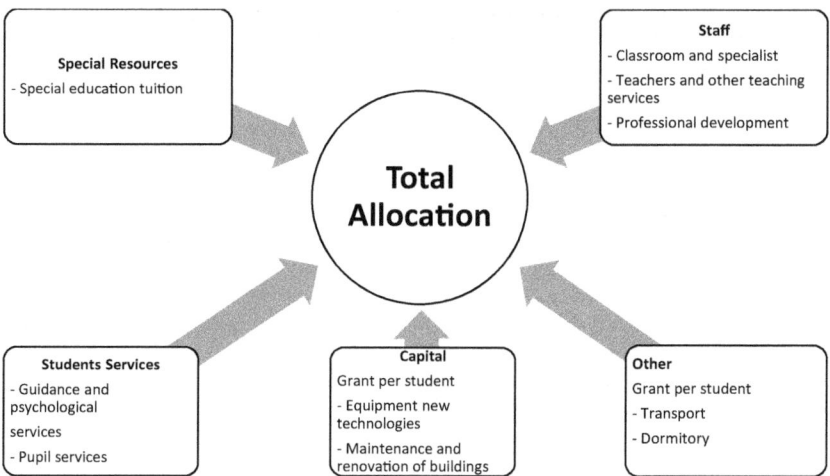

Figure 11: Simplified diagram of the main components of total allocation to school districts in Massachusetts; source: Authors.

Furthermore, to account for most of special needs students, the formula in the state of Massachusetts uses a census model that assumes constant numbers of students with disabilities rather than counting actual enrolments of students. Notably, special education is the only part of the formula that uses this census model because of previous experience with big increases in a number of special needs students (and consequently also in spending on special needs students) over time. On top of that, the state also provides funding for so-called "high-needs" special education students. The funding is expected to pay 75 percent of the cost above the threshold given as four times the average foundation budget per pupil as calculated by the Chapter 70 Aid.

The obvious disadvantage of this system is that it might discriminate against districts with a large share of disabilities. However, this is partly solved by the local contribution, which is calculated based on wealth and income tax, which special education is subject to. Thus, this local contribution indirectly targets special needs students.

This funding formula is very predictable, which makes budgeting of the districts and schools easier. Moreover, it disincentivizes over-identification of students with disabilities.

Below, we summarize some strengths and weaknesses of the funding formula of Massachusetts.

STRENGTHS	WEAKNESSES
1. Consistent and very predictable for school districts as well as for the state, 2. The formula promotes equity as a target local contribution uses local property and income wealth which special education funding is subject to (consequently lower-wealth districts receive more state aid), 3. The formula controls costs for the state as the number of special needs students is fixed, which disincentivizes the over-identification, 4. Flexibility for the districts and motivation to efficiency as the spending is given transparently and there are no specific spending or reporting requirements, 5. The excess cost grant (Special Education Circuit Breaker) limits the possibility of financial difficulties for districts with a higher occurrence of special needs students (that is not assumed by the formula).	1. Cognitive/real injustice for districts with higher occurrence of special needs students than assumed by the formula, 2. Difficult state control over education spending as there is virtually no reporting requirements in place, 3. The increments for districts with high concentrations of low-income students seem to be insufficient at the moment.[56]

---

56 See http://www.doe.mass.edu/finance/chapter70/FBRC-Report.pdf.

Chapter 5
Conclusions

This final chapter summarizes and highlights some features of the funding systems studied. A similar summary of the key features is also provided in Table 21.

Summary of the funding formulas in the selected regions and countries

The five countries and regions studied provide high quality and mostly inclusive education under different jurisdictions and different funding formulas. The majority of the funding is calculated on a per student basis; however, the systems take into account different aspects such as students' or schools' characteristics in order to calculate the total allocation.

For instance, in British Columbia (for details, see Chapter 4.1), the basic allocation is determined by the number of school-age pupils[57] enrolled in a school district. Moreover, the formula takes into account various unique geographic factors and provides supplements for schools in small communities, and it uses a salary differential factor that helps school districts with attracting teachers also in areas with higher salaries and price levels. An interesting feature is that the formula takes into account most of the special needs students and they in general do not receive any extra funding.

Also the Estonian system (see Chapter 4.2) uses 3 basic assumptions: 21 lessons per teacher on average, 24 students per class on average and, on top of the personnel budget, schools receive 20 percent of the personnel budget for resources. The assumptions yield a funding formula that has weighted coefficients that are specific for specific primary and secondary school districts. These coefficients take into account, in some form, the needs of small schools and small classes. They were determined using the previous funding system that turned out to provide too many incentives to keep and/or create small schools. That is why the government in 2012 froze the coefficients. The municipalities have thereby been incentivized to merge schools (as they receive the same amount per student, no matter

---

57 In the calculation of the funding for secondary schools, the number of full-time equivalent pupils is calculated from the number of courses the pupils take (not the actual number of pupils).

the number of schools). The difference between funding for primary and general secondary education is mostly in the coefficients, which are much lower for secondary education Vocational schools are funded based on a simple per student formula where per student allocation changes according to coefficients that differ for different types of training. Finally, the funding formula for special needs students in Estonia is based on the specific class size needs of students, which effectively takes into account the teacher time requirement of students and provides sufficient funding for schools in order to create special classes within mainstream education.

In the Finnish education funding system (Chapter 4.3), municipalities receive funding on a per citizen of school age basis. The municipalities have two main sources of income: transfers from the central government (such as a general allowance, health and social care transfers or culture transfers) and local taxes that are determined by them. These transfers are calculated using various factors such as population, geographical characteristics and socio-economic characteristics. The municipalities' share of co-funding of educational institutions is relatively high in Finland. Finally, only a very limited share of special needs students receives further support (again here the basic per student amounts include funding for most special needs students). This system leads by construction to a reduction in the number of special needs schools and more inclusion of special needs students in the mainstream educational institutions.

Education funding in Flanders (see Chapter 4.4) is more rigorous and complicated compared to the other regions and countries in this book. However, it is also determined mostly on a per student basis. It takes into account the socio-economic status of students and other school and student characteristics (such as the educational attainment of a mother, the language spoken at home etc.). The systems of funding for primary and secondary schools differ significantly (especially compared to British Columbia or Massachusetts). Nevertheless eventually, both funding systems take into account similar characteristics of students and schools. The funding system for secondary schools, furthermore, distinguishes between four tracks. Regarding the funding of special schools, there are two distinct systems. Mainstream schools receive additional funding for special needs students as part of the operations budgets where special needs students co-determine school characteristics that are used to calculate the allocations, and they also receive support from separate special needs schools. The number of integrated students in mainstream education is limited, and currently is the lowest among the EU countries. Separate special schools are funded differently. They receive funding mostly based on the number of students enrolled with respect to the 9 types of special education.

Lastly, the funding formula in the state of Massachusetts (see Chapter 4.5) uses a so-called enrolment foundation which is a count of the number of students for whom a school district is responsible. The enrolment foundation is then multiplied by different cost rates (i.e. different cost rates for different components such as administration or classroom teachers and also for different categories/types such as regular elementary education, secondary education etc.). Furthermore, in order to account for most special needs students, the formula in the state of Massachusetts uses a census model that assumes a constant number of students with disabilities rather than counting actual enrolments of students. Special education is the only part of the formula that uses this census model because of previous experience with significant increases in a number of special needs students (and consequently also in spending on special needs students) over time. On top of that, the state also provides funding for so-called "high-needs" special education students. The obvious disadvantage of this system is that it might discriminate against districts with a large share of disabilities. However, this is partly solved by the local contribution, which is calculated based on wealth and income tax, which special education is subject to, and thus it indirectly targets special needs students. This funding formula is very predictable, which makes the budgeting of the districts and schools easier. Moreover, it disincentivizes over-identification of students with disabilities.

Discussion

The differences in approach to the funding of compulsory education and very good learning outcomes (measured by PISA tests) of the students in these countries and regions suggest that it is not only the funding formula that has an impact on the learning outcomes. The outcomes can also be influenced by the way of dealing with quality issues such as inspections, the self-evaluation of teachers and schools and many other aspects. For example, Estonia uses national exams, sample-based national tests and regular classroom assessments in order to assess student performance. Such tests and school inspections were often found to be positively associated with students' learning outcomes (Mathew and Sammons, 2004; Luginbuhl et al., 2009; McCrone et al. 2009). Nevertheless, we can observe some features of the funding systems that seem to be successful in pursuing particular policy goals, and we can also identify some features common to the funding formulas in the well-performing countries.

One of the main challenges that appeared in the studied formulas for compulsory education is how to deal with small and rural schools or with a decline in the number of students and school sizes. As can be seen from the example of Estonia, when an additional allocation for small classes depends only on the number of students in the schools (in order to support small rural schools), the system quickly becomes very costly. And thus, consequently, Estonia had to change the allocation formula so that funding no longer increases if the school becomes smaller. Generally, the formula used in British Columbia is a more suitable solution and a good source of inspiration on how to deal with such issues. A simpler alternative is the formula that is used in the district of Mission. This funding formula provides additional allocations based on geographical distances (or alternatively traveling distances) to other closest schools (or similarly to the sparseness factor). This makes the allocation less prone to incentivize the existence of small schools that could easily merge and, at the same time, it keeps the traveling distance for students at the level desired by the government.

With respect to equity in education, a common challenge for education funding formulas is how to deal with vulnerable students, such as students coming from disadvantaged socio-economic backgrounds or immigration backgrounds. There are at least two approaches to include these factors in the funding formulas. First, some countries and regions (e.g. British Columbia, Flanders or Massachusetts) provide higher allocations for students who are identified as vulnerable. Second, some countries and regions fund schools in an indirect way. In particular, they use socio-economic characteristics to calculate general transfers to the municipalities (e.g. in Finland). These general transfers include transfers for education, but also for housing, social policies, infrastructure, etc. The municipalities can then decide on the share of this general transfer that is allocated to the school (e.g., in Massachusetts[58]). There are some advantages of this approach compared to the systems where schools are directly compensated for disadvantaged students. First, it increases the commitment of municipalities to education. Second, it ensures that the municipalities have some choice[59] and motivation regarding the efficient provision of education (for example, municipalities can provide incentives

---

58 A similar system is due to be put in place also in Estonia from 2019. The government has already decided that and at the moment we are making preparations to distribute all the funding to municipalities through their income tax revenues and equalization fund. The municipalities will have full responsibilities for deciding the funding of education, as is done in all other Nordic countries.

59 The solutions are very unlikely to be universally the same for a whole country to get to the same results.

for small schools to merge into larger school boards). Situations where extra funding is required (e.g. if there are few students in a school or in rural areas) should already be resolved beforehand at the level of the equalization fund with no (or no direct) connection to educational decisions made by the municipalities afterwards. Third, this avoids the incentive for over-identification of vulnerable students at the level of schools. To avoid an annual decrease in the real budget, the lump sum amounts paid to the municipalities should ideally be inflation-indexed only every year (as in Massachusetts).

One of the main challenges of the funding formulas for secondary schools is how to deal with different tracks. In British Columbia and Massachusetts, where secondary education is a part of a single framework of so-called K-12 education, the funding formula is in large part identical (the structure is the same, the specific allocations might differ) to the formula for primary education. This is in contrast to the system in continental Europe where there is often a completely different system for secondary education (Flanders), or at least a different system for vocational tracks in secondary education (Estonia and Finland). The former system (i.e. an identical calculation for primary and secondary schools) appears more advisable as it simplifies the whole funding system, and thus also lowers costs for administrative bodies (since then budgeting would follow the same process; see also the report by The Assembly Higher Education Committee (2003)[60] that identifies ease of understanding as one of the main principles in designing funding formulas). Especially in countries where school boards/districts govern both primary and secondary schools and have budgetary autonomy, one unified funding system is more appropriate and is likely to bring savings and the same outcomes.

Regarding special needs students, we can see that the funding models have been rapidly changing in recent years (see the cases of Estonia, Finland or Flanders). One of the common reasons why these formulas have changed is identification of special needs students, i.e. the number of students identified as students with special needs has been increasing dramatically. Thus, a simple formula based on the number of students identified as special needs students has become more and more expensive. The common approach to overcome this issue was to include a majority of students with disabilities or special needs already in the basic per student allocation (which is the case in Finland, British Columbia or Massachusetts). There are at least two advantages to this approach. First, it does not incentivize the over-identification of recipients of

---

60 The Assembly Higher Education Committee identified the following 10 principles: Adequacy of funding, Equity of funding, Stability of funding, Link to state priorities, Easy to understand, Affordability for students, Cost sharing, Accountability, Accessibility.

such funding.[61] This makes the system less costly and should lead to a decline or at least a slower increase in the number of new special needs students. Second, it leads to a reduction in the creation of special schools since it rather incentivizes school districts or municipalities either to create special classes or to include them completely in mainstream education as they do not receive any extra funds for such students. For instance, in Massachusetts, a fixed share of students with disabilities in the population is assumed[62] and some special funds are provided in order to partially reimburse the differences between the actual expenses and the assumed allocation that is computed on a per student basis.

At the same time, it appears necessary to keep special funding for a limited group of severely disabled students. In this aspect, there are two approaches: *i)* the additional funds can be spent directly by the school districts that would hire educational assistants so that the students can then attend mainstream schools with the help of the assistant; or *ii)* the funds can be sent to the school which then needs to hire more staff to be able to satisfy the special needs. An interesting way to compute funding for these students is the funding formula for special needs which is based on the specific class size needs of special needs students. Using this approach, the additional funding can easily be calculated from the teacher time requirement of students (as in Estonia where a regular full class consists of 24 students and it can go up to 1 student per teacher for most severely disabled students). For instance, a student that needs to be in a class of a maximum of 8 students would generate a funding of approximately 2.5 times the basic allocation for mainstream students (assuming a standard class of 20 students) and a student that needs one-to-one teaching would generate 15 times the basic allocation for the mainstream students. As you can see, the proposed mechanism (as well as the one used in Estonia) is degressive, i.e., the funding for most severe disabilities covers a lower share of the actual costs than the funding for lighter disabilities. This, furthermore, disincentivizes over-identification of the most severe disabilities.

There are also a few concerns with the aforementioned approach. First, if there is free enrolment in schools (such as in Flanders) – i.e. parents can freely choose a school – and schools have some power to select students, then

---

61 For instance, in Finland the number of students with special needs that generated additional funding for schools increased from 15 to 30 percent between 2001 and 2010. After the majority of such students was included in the basic allocation, the number of special needs students started to decline again.

62 Specifically, it is assumed that the incidence of special needs is about 14 percent and such students receive special needs services on average 25 percent of the time, which results in a 3.5 percent fixed share of full-time equivalent special needs students.

there is an incentive for schools to try to avoid more costly (i.e. disabled) students. A targeted policy can avoid this selection of students. Second, fewer students in special education schools due to inclusive education may lead to higher average costs in these (less populated) special education schools – i.e. separate special schools might benefit from economies of scale. If more pupils with special needs are spread over mainstream schools, these pupils generate some additional teaching/assisting hours for the main-stream schools. However, engaging specific teachers or paramedic staff for a small number of hours (e.g. for 1 or 2 students) may be difficult and not cost-effective. This is less of a problem either in larger inclusive schools when additional hours for special needs students can be pooled and used more efficiently or when the specialized staff is hired directly by a school district and not the schools them-selves and can, thus, be pooled. The network of special needs teachers that supports the mainstream schools also makes this issue less important as it reduces cost-efficiency losses because the specific teachers or paramedic staff have duties also in the mainstream schools.

In some education systems (British Columbia and Massachusetts), we see extra funding for gifted students. In British Columbia, the funding of such students is now included in the basic allocation and teachers receive guidelines on how to approach them. In Massachusetts, a very limited program of discretionary grants was discontinued in 2010. The experience suggests that any extra funding calculated on a per enrolled student basis could lead to over-identification. Thus, we would recommend the promotion and development of a special approach (such as special instruction and voluntary groups etc.) to the gifted students within the basic per student allocation for mainstream education.

Overall, we suggest that any funding formula should take into account at least the following compensating factors: compensation for geographical differences, vulnerable students and salary differences. These factors should be used together with other factors to determine lump sum allocations (non-earmarked transfers) to school boards that would then decide on funding for particular schools in a given school board. Lump sum allocations have the advantage that they increase the policy making power of schools, such that school managers can better develop their own policies and adapt the expenses to local needs. This increases the efficiency of the spending (i.e. expenses will only be made if there is a local need, and not because of some centrally decided policy which might be irrelevant for a particular school). By providing the school boards and not the schools directly with the funding, economies of scale can be achieved at the school board level. This is attractive as the school board can then develop its own administration, which takes specific and generic administrative duties away from the schools. Again, this can increase the policy making power of the school as the school manager can better concentrate on his/her core tasks. However, in systems with earmarked educational grants, a simple transformation of the earmarked grant into non-earmarked would likely lead to very similar results as the earmarked grant. Experience shows that better results are achieved in those countries that aggregated many different grants to this lump sum funding (such as Finland and other Nordic countries) as this cuts or blurs the connections between the factors that determine the funding and the spending itself. This is important since then the school boards can plan education spending on their own and according to their needs which is likely to lead to efficiency and well-suited policies.

As a final remark, we note that it is important to focus also on outcomes (e.g., the self-evaluation of schools and teachers) instead of just inputs. The earmarking of allocations to schools or school districts is only one element of input control. If the education system concentrated on inputs, it might overlook the importance of monitoring the outputs and using this knowledge to build up relevant measures. Furthermore, the monitoring systems should ideally orientate on counseling rather than simple controlling since the school (boards) will get more powers as well as responsibilities. Lastly, it is necessary to point out that in the case of the transfer of many resources to municipalities, it has to be very clear what institution is responsible; shared or unclear responsibilities are unlikely to lead to the desired outcomes.

Finally, we would like to point to some future research endeavors. Our work could easily be extended in terms of regions covered in our analysis; however, there are many more possibilities. Firstly, our analysis does not cover the efficiency implications of various funding formulas and efficiency is certainly an interesting aspect of the formulas to study. Secondly, the funding formulas can be examined quantitatively to analyze to what extent they promote equity. This is apparent, for instance, in the case of Flanders where there exists a quite extensive system of support for disadvantaged students. However, this book has not analyzed to what extent this additional funding actually improves the educational outcomes of disadvantaged students. Furthermore, the current funding systems often do provide some additional funding for disadvantaged students; however, they do not fully take into account the fact that the schools with a large share of those students often cannot attract the best, experienced teachers, and thus employ young, less experienced teachers, which can further lead to worse performance. Additional funding to attract more experienced teachers might improve the situation. Thirdly, there are now a number of reforms in a similar direction such as the transition from ear-marked funds to lump sum funding. These reforms can be examined quantitatively in a cross-country study to get to know which reforms lead to better educational outcomes. Fourthly, many countries and regions, especially in Europe and Northern America, face the issue of costly small schools in less populated areas. We comment on this issue especially in the case studies on British Columbia and Estonia. However, this topic deserves more attention from scholars. It remains largely open which strategy is the best and what the impacts of the current strategies are on the educational outcomes and the efficiency of education spending. Fifthly, the trade between inclusion and efficiency of education of students with special needs has not to the best of our knowledge been studied. Lastly, as we did not attempt to develop an analytical framework to analyze the funding system in general, such a framework can be an important contribution to the literature.

Appendix

Tables 19-22

	British Columbia	Estonia	Finland	Flanders	Massa-chusetts	OECD average
Expenditure on educational institution [on GDP]	5.7*	5.2	5.7	5.8**	6.2***	5.2
Share of young population [less than 15 years old]	16.1*	15.8	16.4	17.0**	19.2***	X
Share of public expenditure on primary education	92*	98	100	97**	93***	93
Share of public expenditure on lower secondary education	92*	98	100	96**	92***	93
Annual expenditure per student in primary school (USD in PPP)	9,130*	7,138	8,519	9,957**	10,959***	8,412
Annual expenditure per student in secondary school (USD in PPP)	X	6,417	10,237	12,763**	12,740***	9,751

Table 19: Spending on education in the chosen regions and countries, the share of the young is reported as of 2014; notes: * figures for the whole of Canada, ** for Belgium. *** for the United States, X figures not available; source: own representation of OECD (2016, 2019).

	British Columbia	Estonia	Finland	Flanders	Massachusetts	OECD average
Index of school responsibility for resource allocation	-0.35*	0.14	-0.28	-0.29**	0.08***	-0.05
Index of school autonomy over curricula and assessments	-0.49*	0.49	-0.05	-0.11**	-0.39***	-0.04

Table 20: Indices of school responsibilities for resource allocation and over curricula and assessments as measures of school autonomy countries. The higher index, the higher autonomy in the respective area; notes: * figures for the whole of Canada, ** for Belgium. *** for the United States; source: own representation of OECD (2013).

	British Columbia	Estonia	Finland	Flanders	Massachusetts
Type of funding model	Per Capita	Per Capita	Per Capita***	Per capita	Hybrid of Resourced-based and Per Capita
Additional factors on top of the basic formula	Unique and vulnerable students, geographic factors	Fixed coefficients based on assumed number of classes, isolated and sparsely populated areas supplements	Morbidity, unemployment, number of other than Finnish speaking, Swedish/Saame speaking, archipelago	Socio-economic status of students, Brussels supplement, sparsely populated areas, non-Dutch speaking students	Wage adjustment factor Economically disadvantaged status
Type of funding model for special needs	Per Capita	Per Capita**	Per Capita**** (mostly included in Basic Allocation)	Per Capita	Included in Basic Allocation + Excess cost grants
Main components of funding formula	Salaries of teachers and school principals, in-service training, educational assistants, first nation resource workers, transport, capital spending.*	Salaries of teachers and school directors, professional development of teachers and school directors, school lunches, study materials	To be decided by the providers of education that receive lump-sum amounts.	Teaching staff, replacement units for teachers' absences, school principals, operations budgets	Administration, instructional leadership, classroom and specialist teachers, other teaching services, professional development, instructional equipment and technology, guidance and psychological services, pupil services, operations and maintenance employee, benefits and fixed charges, special education tuition

Table 21: Overview of funding types and their characteristics in the chosen regions and countries; notes: * the components are described in the case of the district of Mission, ** the formula takes into account the number of special needs students with a given severe disability in class, *** based on the number of school-age children, not the actual enrollment, **** note that this is limited to a very small group students; source: Authors.

	British Columbia	Estonia	Finland	Flanders	Massachusetts
Share of special needs students	10.6 %	4.4 %*	7.5 %**	6.63 %***	17,56 %

Table 22: Shares of special needs students in 2016/2017 in the chosen regions and countries; the figures cannot be easily compared as the definitions in respective countries might differ; notes: * in 2013/2014, ** students in Tier 3, *** in 2012; source: Authors.

The types of education classes in the Flemish Community

a) the first year of the A stream and the second year of the first cycle[63];
b) the first year of the B stream and the pre-vocational year;
c) the reception years;
d) the second and third cycles A.S.O.[64];
e) the second and third cycles T.S.O.[65], with the proviso that a distinction is made between the following groups of disciplines:
   1. Administration and distribution, Sport;
   2. Chemistry, Industrial techniques, Agriculture and horticulture, Paramedical training, Personal care, Nutrition;
   3. Hotel, Clothing and clothing;
   4. Electricity;
   5. Decorative techniques, Graphic techniques;
   6. Social safety, Optics, Orthopedic techniques, Dental techniques, Care techniques;
   7. Timber and construction, Metal, Rhine and inland shipping, Textiles;
   8. Glass techniques;
f) the second and third cycles B.S.O.[66] and HBO nursing, on the understanding that a distinction is made between the following groups of disciplines:
   1. Administration and distribution, Sport;
   2. Social security, Agriculture and horticulture, Personal care;
   3. Decorative techniques, Electricity, Hotel;
   4. Clothing and confection, Care techniques;
   5. Graphic techniques;
   6. Glass processing, Gold jewelry, Wood and construction, Marble working, Metal, Rhine and inland shipping, Textiles;
   7. Truck driver;
   8. Nursing;
g) the second and third cycles K.S.O.[67], with the proviso that a distinction is made between the following groups of disciplines:
   1. Visual arts;
   2. Word;
   3. Dance;
   4. Music

---

63 Here, a cycle means 2 years of education and there are 3 cycles in secondary schools (6 years in total).
64 General secondary education.
65 Technical secondary education.
66 Vocational secondary education.
67 Art secondary education.

Overview of the coefficients for teaching hours per student in the Flemish Community

1. for the course years referred to in Appendix "The types of education classes" a):
   - in the bracket from 1 to 25 pupils: 2.25
   - in the bracket from 26 up to and including 50 pupils: 1.95
   - in the bracket from 51 to 100 pupils: 1.80
   - from the 101st student: 1.60
2. for the course years referred to in Appendix "The types of education classes" b):
   - in the bracket from 1 to 25 pupils: 3.05
   - in the bracket from 26 to 50 pupils: 2.75
   - in the bracket from 51 up to and including 100 pupils: 2.60
   - from the 101st student: 2.45
3. for the course years referred to in Appendix "The types of education classes" c):
   - in the bracket from 1 to 25 pupils: 2.25
   - in the bracket from 26 up to and including 50 pupils: 1.95
   - in the bracket from 51 to 100 pupils: 1.80
   - from the 101st student: 1.60
4. for the years of education referred to in Appendix "The types of education classes" d), applied separately on the one hand to pupils of the second degree, on the other hand to pupils of the third degree:
   - in the bracket from 1 to 25 pupils: 1.90
   - in the bracket from 26 to 50 pupils: 1.70
   - in the bracket from 51 up to and including 100 pupils: 1.60
   - from the 101st student: 1.45
5. for the course years referred to in Appendix "The types of education classes" e), applied separately to students of the second degree, on the other hand to students of the third degree:
   - group 1 °: 2.05
   - group 2 °: 2.15
   - group 3 °: 2.25
   - group 4 °: 2.35
   - group 5 °: 2.45
   - group 6 °: 2.55
   - group 7 °: 2.65
   - group 8 °: 2.75

An increase is, however, granted for the total of pupils in groups 1° to 8°, applied separately on the one hand on the second degree, on the other hand on the third degree:
- in the bracket from 1 to 25 pupils: 0.50
- in the bracket from 26 up to and including 75 pupils: 0.30
- in the bracket from 76 to 150 pupils: 0.10
- from the 151th student: none

6. for the course years referred to in Appendix "The types of education classes" (f), applied separately to pupils of the second degree, to pupils of the third degree, and to students of HBO nursing:
   - group 1°: 2.45
   - group 2°: 2.55
   - group 3°: 2.65
   - group 4°: 2.75
   - group 5°: 2.85
   - group 6°: 3.05
   - group 7°: 3.70
   - group 8°: 3.80

An increase is, however, granted for the total of the pupils of groups 1° to 7° (i.e. not group 8°), applied separately to the second degree and to the third degree:
- in the bracket from 1 to 25 pupils: 0.60
- in the bracket from 26 up to and including 75 pupils: 0.30
- in the bracket from 76 to 150 pupils: 0.15
- from the 151th student: nil

7. for the course years referred to in Appendix "The types of education classes" (g), applied separately on the one hand on the second degree, on the other hand on the third degree:
   - group 1°: 2.70
   - group 2°: 2.70
   - group 3°: 2.70
   - group 4°: 2.70

However, a further increase is granted for the relevant degree:
a) for schools outside the K.S.O. offering other types of education in the second degree:
- in the bracket from 1 to 25 pupils: 0.50
- in the bracket from 26 up to and including 75 pupils: 0.30
- in the bracket from 76 to 150 pupils: 0.10
- from the 151st student: none

b) for schools outside the K.S.O. offering other types of education in the third grade:
  - in the bracket from 1 to 25 pupils: 0.50
  - in the bracket from 26 up to and including 75 pupils: 0.30
  - in the bracket from 76 to 150 pupils: 0.10
  - from the 151th student: none
  c) for schools outside the K.S.O. offering no other forms of education in the second degree:
  - group 1°: 0.20
  - group 2°: 1.20
  - group 3°: 1.20
  - group 4°: 2.20
  d) for schools outside the K.S.O. not offering any other forms of education in the third degree:
  - group 1°: 0.20
  - group 2°: 1.20
  - group 3°: 1.20
  - group 4°: 2.20

  Contrary to the foregoing and irrespective of whether or not the school in the relevant degree offers other types of education outside the K.S.O., the increase for the structure components of Music and Special musical education is always 2.20. Where appropriate, the pupils concerned shall be disregarded in the application of the provisions under (a) or (b).
8. for schools belonging to a school community and located in the administrative district of Brussels capital on the one hand, and for schools located in municipalities whose population density is lower than 125 inhabitants per km²:
   - the coefficients referred to in 1°, 2° and 3°, increased by 0.10;
   the coefficients referred to in 4° and the coefficients of the groups referred to in 5°, 6° and 7°, increased by 0.20.

Figures 12-16

Key

⇧/△ Starting/ending age of compulsory education

▲ Recognized exit point of the education system

↑ Typical student flow

↑ (dashed) Transfer from a programme to another

▭ (pink) Programme designed for part-time attendance

▭ (white) Vocational/Professional orientation
(according to national definition at the tertiary level)

▭ (grey border) Single structure education (integrated ISCED levels)

┊ May be provided within one school structure

⊥ (with arc) Transfer at crossing lines is not possible

Diploma Name of diploma, degree or certificate

2018 Reference year (school year 2017/2018 in the northern hemisphere)

* **Theoretical starting ages** refer to the ages as established by law and regulation for the entry to a programme, actual starting ages may vary depending on the programme.

 http://gpseducation.oecd.org/

APPENDIX

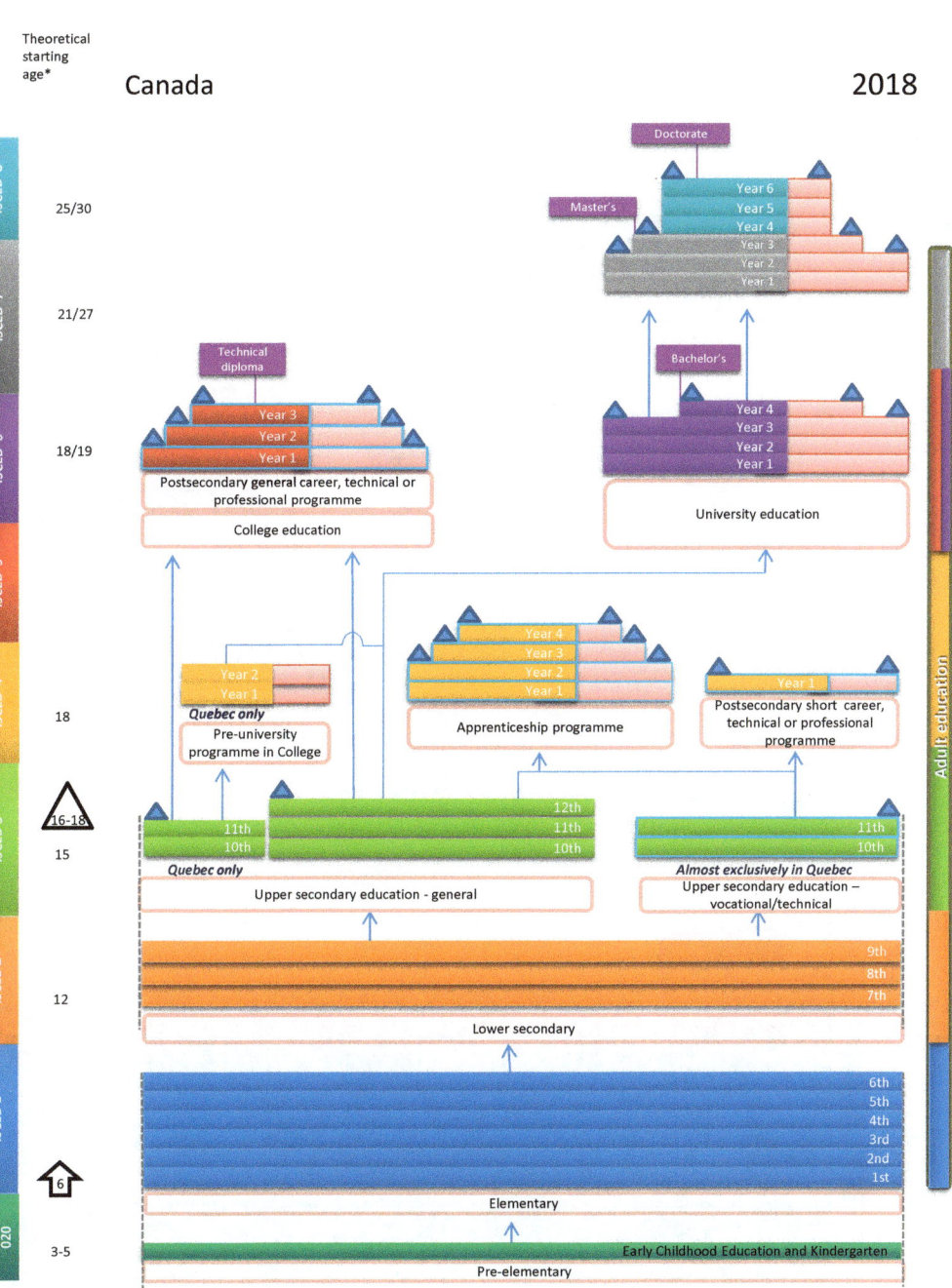

Figure 12: Structure of education system in Canada; source: http://gpseducation.oecd.org/CountryProfile?primaryCountry=CAN.

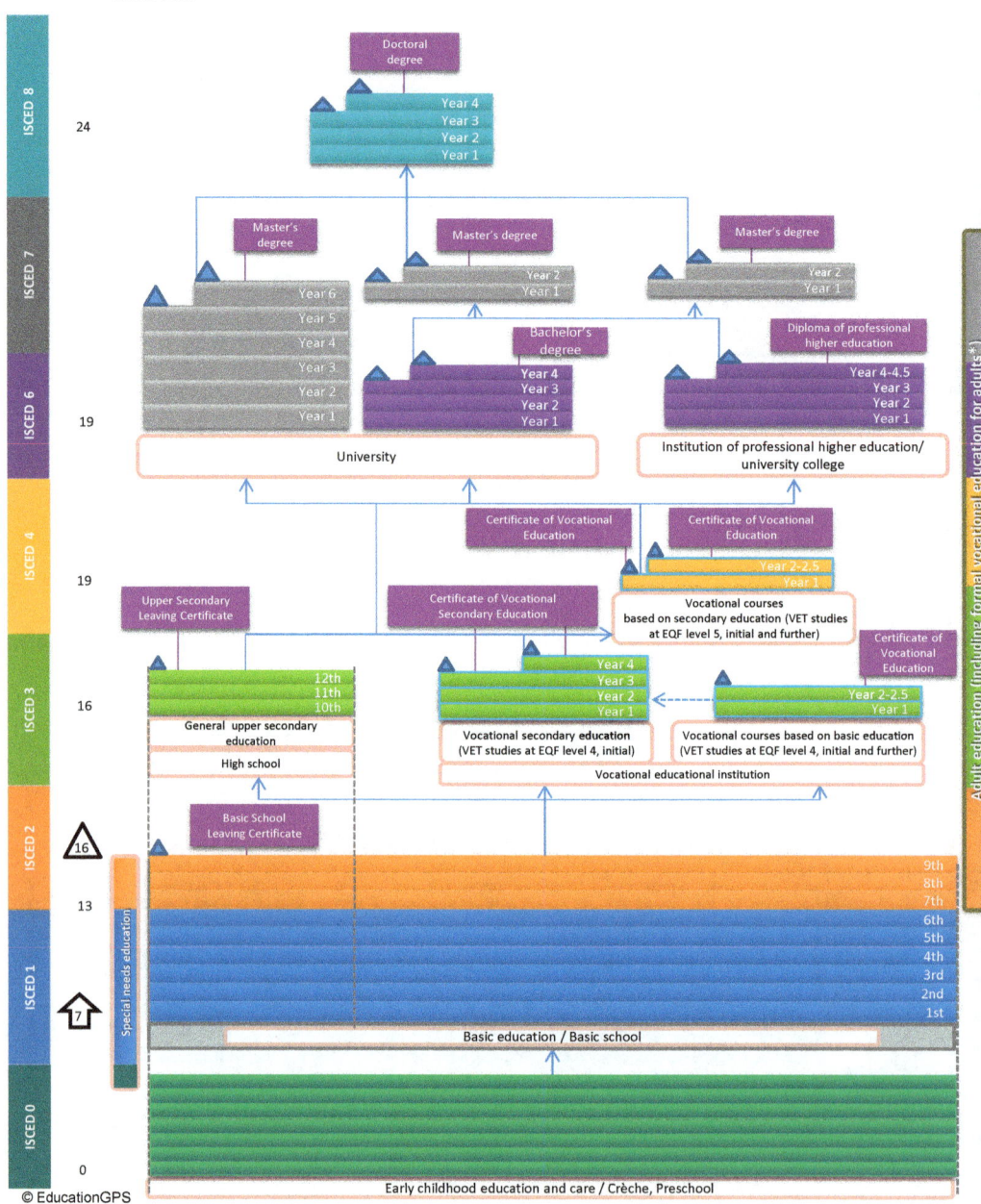

Figure 13: Structure of the education system in Estonia; source: http://gpseducation.oecd.org/CountryProfile?primaryCountry=EST.

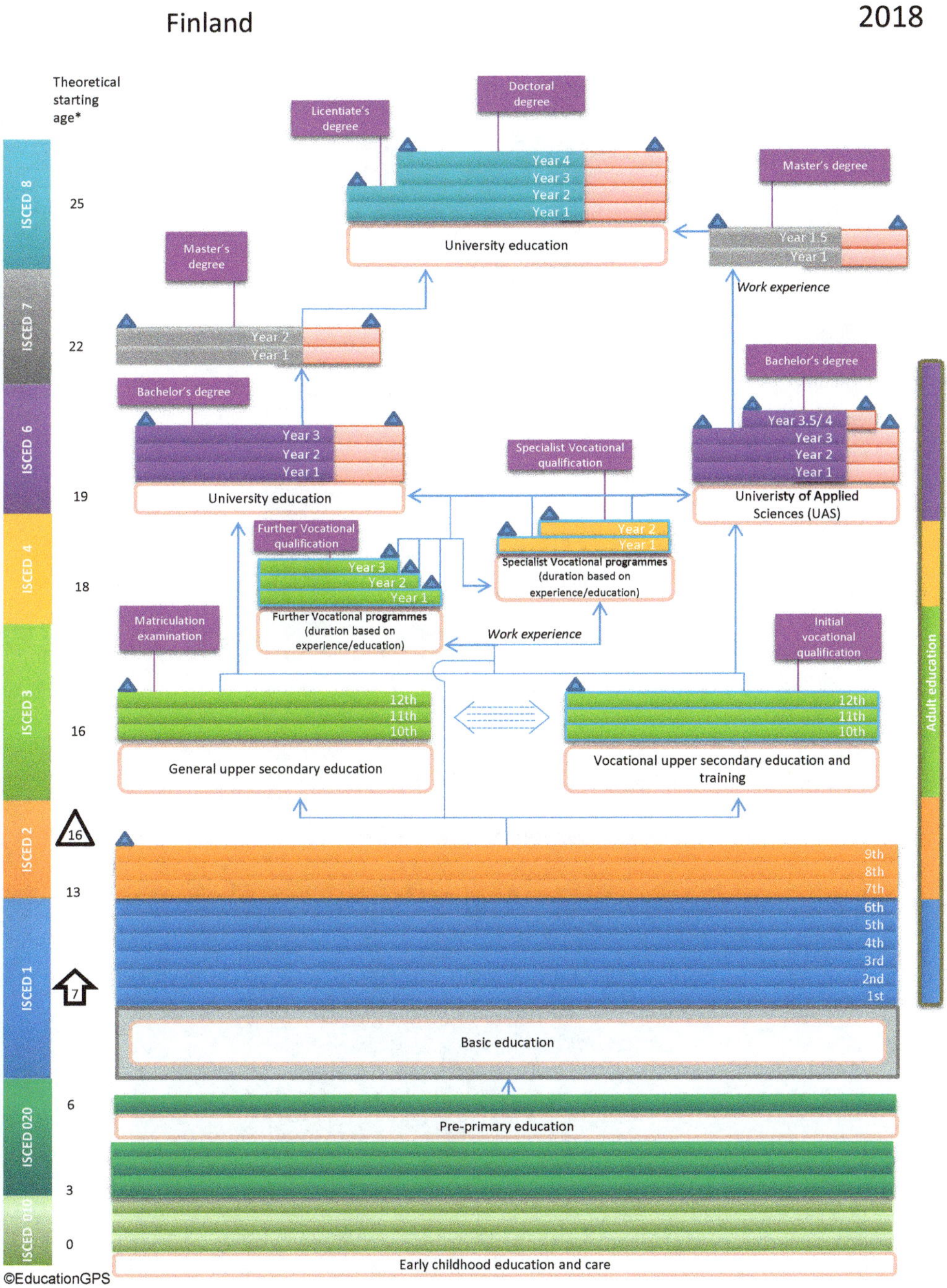

APPENDIX

Finland   2018

Figure 14: Structure of the education system in Finland; source: http://gpseducation.oecd.org/CountryProfile?primaryCountry=FIN.

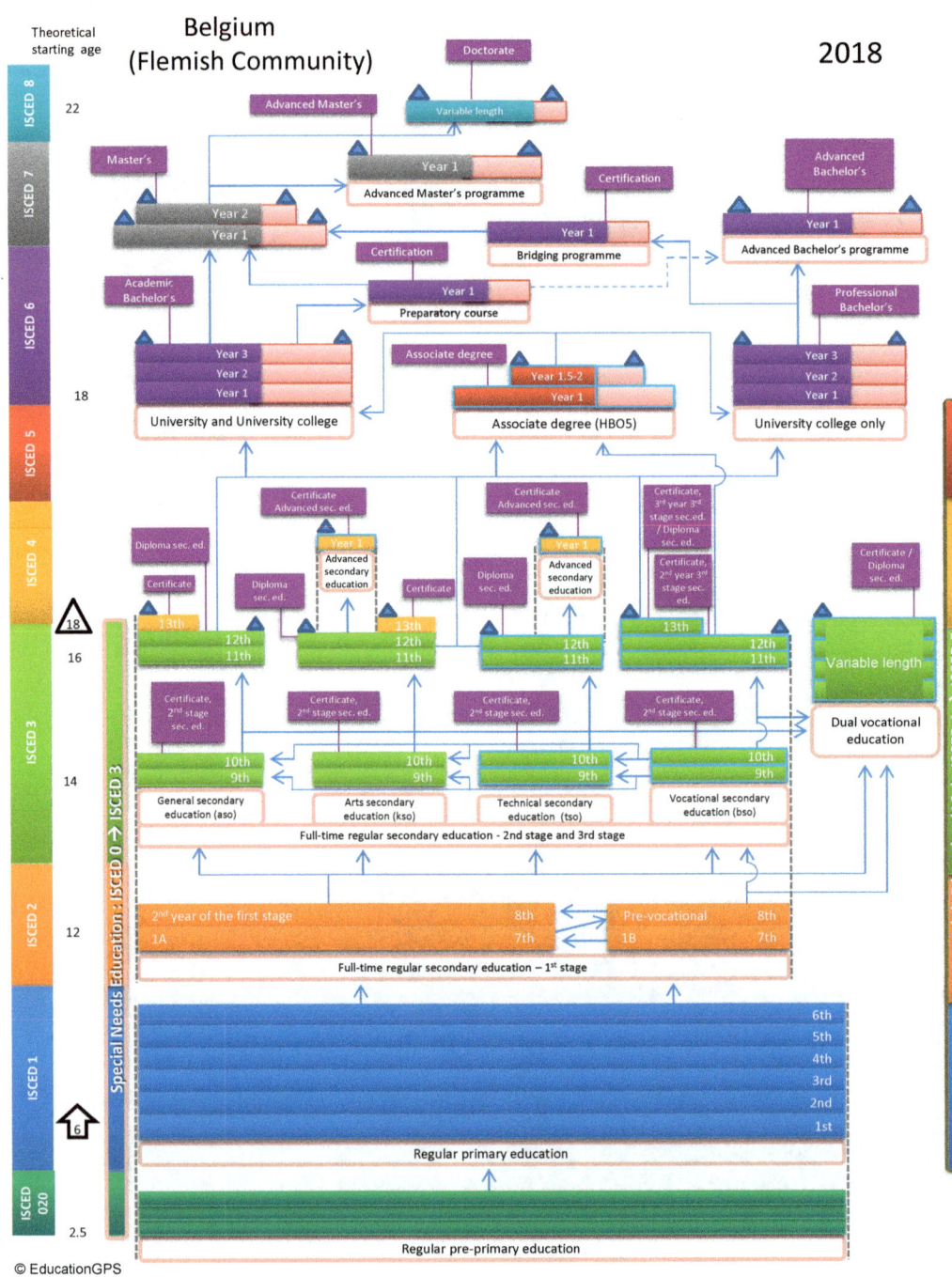

Figure 15: Structure of the education system in Flanders; source: http://gpseducation.oecd.org/CountryProfile?primaryCountry=BFL.

APPENDIX

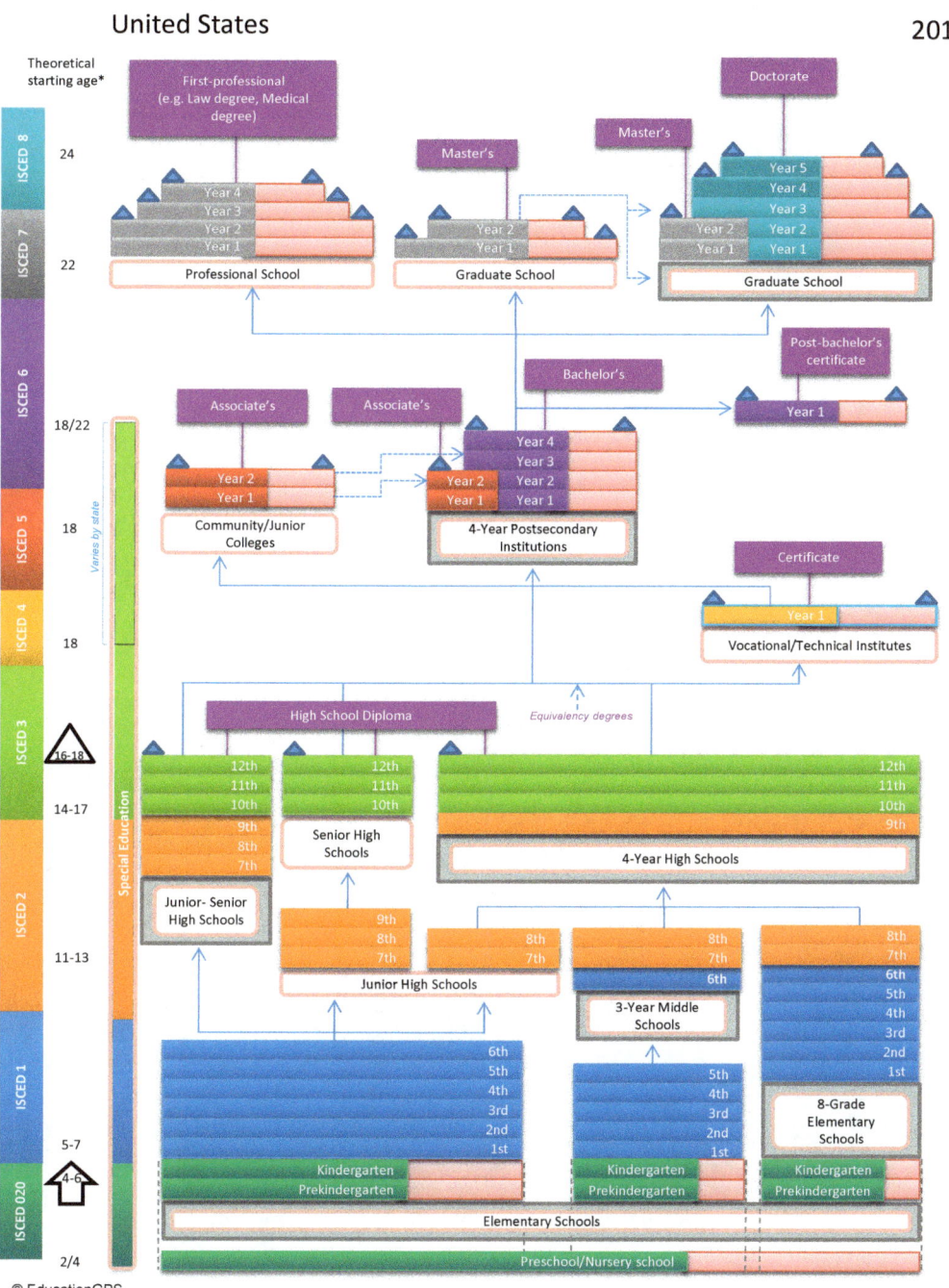

Figure 16: Structure of the education system in the USA; source: http://gpseducation.oecd.org/CountryProfile?primaryCountry=USA.

List of primary sources

This list provides an overview of some primary sources for each of the countries and regions studied. We refer to some insightful operating manuals, laws or research articles. Due to the specificity of the content, some of the sources are presented in their original language. All links were operational on October 9, 2017.

British Columbia

1. Provincial funding of school districts
   § British Columbia, Resource Management Division (2016). *2016/17 Operating Grants Manual.* Available at: http://www.fnesc.ca/wp/wp-content/uploads/2015/06/16-17-operating-grants-manual.pdf.
   § British Columbia, Resource Management Division (2017). *Overview of the 2017/18 Operating Grant Allocation Formula.* Available at: http://www2.gov.bc.ca/assets/gov/education/administration/resource-management/k12funding/17-18/17-18-overview.pdf.
2. Policies, procedures, and guidelines that support the delivery of special education services
   § British Columbia, Special Education Services (2016). *A Manual of Policies, Procedures and Guidelines.* Available at: http://www2.gov.bc.ca/assets/gov/education/administration/kindergarten-to-grade-12/inclusive/special_ed_policy_manual.pdf.

Estonia

1. Coefficients for the calculation of funding for municipal and city general education schools
   § RiigiTeataja.ee (2017). *Valdade ja linnade üldhariduskoolide toetuse arvestamise aluseks olevad koefitsiendid.* Available at: https://www.riigiteataja.ee/aktilisa/1050/7201/7020/VV_16m_lisa1.pdf (in Estonian).
2. A detailed description of the funding formula from 2008 (used to compute fixed coefficients in 2014)

§ Levačić, R. (2011). Per capita financing of education in Estonia, in J.D. Alonso and A. Sanchez (eds.) (2011), *Reforming Education Finance in Six Transition Countries: Six Case Studies in Per Capita Financing Systems*, Chapter 3, The World Bank, Washington, DC. Available at: http://elibrary.worldbank.org/doi/abs/10.1596/ 978-0-8213-8783-2#.
3. A general overview of school resources in Estonia by the OECD
   § Santiago, P. et al. (2016). *OECD Reviews of School Resources: Estonia 2016*. OECD Reviews of School Resources. Paris: OECD Publishing.

Finland

1. Acts regulating education provision and transfers from the central government to municipalities
   - Basic Education Act (642/2010). Finnish Ministry of Culture and Education. Available at: http://www.finlex.fi/en/laki/kaannokset/1998/en19980628.pdf (with amendment available at: http://www.oph.fi/download/132551_amendments_and_additions_to_national_core_curriculum_basic_education.pdf)
   - Act on Funding for Teaching and Cultural Activities (1705/2009). Finnish Ministry of Culture and Education. Available at: http://www.finlex.fi/sv/laki/ajantasa/2009/20091705#a30.12.2014-1410 (in Swedish).
2. Overview of the coefficients and allocation for the calculation of transfers to municipalities
   - Finnish Ministry of Education (2016). *Opetus- ja kulttuuritoimen rahoituslain (1705/2009) perusteella rahoitettavan esi- ja perusopetuksen yksikköhinnat vuonna 2017*. Available at: https://vos.oph.fi/rap/vos/v17/v05yk6y17.pdf (in Finnish)

Flanders

1. Circulars and the acts on basic education and its funding.
   - Vlaamse Overheid. (1997). Decreet basisonderwijs. Brussel: Vlaamse Overheid. Available at: https://data-onderwijs.vlaanderen.be/edulex/document.aspx?docid=12254 (in Dutch).
   - Vlaamse Overheid. (1998). Het werkingsbudget in het basisonderwijs. Brussel: Vlaamse Overheid. Available at: https://data-onderwijs.vlaanderen.be/edulex/document.aspx?docid=9437 (in Dutch).

- Vlaamse Overheid. (2005). Personeelsformatie Scholen in het Gewoon Basisonderwijs. Brussel: Vlaamse Overheid. Vlaamse Overheid. (2016). Available at: http://data-onderwijs.vlaanderen.be/edulex/document.aspx?docid=13615 (in Dutch).
2. Circulars on special education
    - Vlaamse Overheid. (2017). Het ondersteuningsmodel in het basis- en secundair onderwijs en in het hoger onderwijs. Brussel: Vlaamse Overheid. Available at: http://data-onderwijs.vlaanderen.be/edulex/document.aspx?docid=15071 (in Dutch).

Massachusetts

1. The Basic Act
    - The Commonwealth of Massachusetts. General Law *Chapter 70: SCHOOL FUNDS AND STATE AID FOR PUBLIC SCHOOLS.* Available at: https://malegislature.gov/Laws/GeneralLaws/PartI/TitleXII/Chapter70.
2. Funding and Foundation Enrolment calculation
    - Massachusetts Department of Elementary and Secondary Education (2017). *The Massachusetts Foundation Budget.* Available at: http://www.doe.mass.edu/finance/chapter70/chapter-cal.pdf.
    - Massachusetts Department of Elementary and Secondary Education (2017). Foundation Enrollment. Available at: http://www.doe.mass.edu/finance/chapter70/enrollment-desc.pdf.
3. Act on special education
    - Massachusetts Department of Elementary and Secondary Education. *603 CMR 28.00: Special Education.* Available at: http://www.doe.mass.edu/lawsregs/603cmr28.html?section=all.

References

Alexander, N. A. (2004). *Exploring the changing face of Adequacy.* Peabody Journal of Education, 79(3).
Baker, B.D. (2018). *Educational Inequality and School Finance: Why Money Matters for America's Students.* Harvard Education Press, MA: Cambridge.
BenDavid-Hadar, I. (ed.) (2018). *Education Finance, Equality, and Equity.* Springer International Publishing, New York: New York City.
Blaton, L. (2008). *Geschiedenis van het steunpunt GOK. Opgehaald van Steunpuntgok.be:* http://www.steunpuntgok.be/over_steunpunt_gelijke_onderwijskansen/geschiedenis/ [accessed on 02/01/2017].
Booth, T. (2000). Controlling the agenda: policies on inclusion and exclusion in England. In *Policy, Contexts and Comparative Perspectives* ed. by Armstrong, D., Armstrong, F. and Barton, L. London: Fulton.
British Columbia, Ministry of Education (2016a). *Newcomer Welcome Letter – 2016.* Available at http://www2.gov.bc.ca/assets/gov/education/administration/kindergarten-to-grade-12/diverse-student-needs/educationwelcomeletter_jan2016_english_final.pdf [accessed on 02/08/2017]. Victoria: Ministry of Education.
British Columbia, Ministry of Education (2016b). *Student Statistics – 2016/17.* Available at http://www.bced.gov.bc.ca/reports/pdfs/student_stats/prov.pdf [accessed on 02/08/2017]. Victoria: Ministry of Education.
British Columbia, Special Education Services (2016). *A Manual of Policies, Procedures and Guidelines.* Victoria: Ministry of Education.
British Columbia Teachers' Federation (2012). *2012 BC Education Facts.* Vancouver.
Cedefop (2017). *Vocational education and training in Estonia: short description.* Available at http://dx.doi.org/10.2801/15844 [accessed on 02/01/2018]. Luxembourg: Publications Office.
Children's Law Center of Massachusetts (2013). *Special Education in Massachusetts.* Available at http://www.clcm.org/Special_Education_in_MA_Feb2013.pdf [accessed on 02/08/2017]. MA: Lynn.
Connecticut School Finance Project (2016). *Improving How Connecticut Funds Special Education.* CT: New Haven.
Cornman, S.Q., and Zhou, L. (2016). *Revenues and Expenditures for Public Elementary and Secondary Education: School Year 2013–14 (Fiscal Year 2014)* (NCES 2016-301). U.S. Department of Education. Washington, DC: National Center for Education Statistics. Retrieved [09/08/2017] from http://nces.ed.gov/pubsearch.
Council of Ministers of Education, Canada. (2016). *Measuring up: Canadian Results of the OECD PISA Study.* Ontario: Council of Ministers of Education, Canada.
De Witte, K. and Hindriks, J. (2017). *De Geslaagde School – L'école de la réussite.* Itinera book.
Espinoza, O. (2007). *Solving the equity–equality conceptual dilemma: a new model for analysis of the educational process.* Educational Research. 49(4), 343–363.
European Agency for Development in Special Needs Education, 2012. *Special Needs Education Country Data 2012,* Odense: European Agency for Development in Special Needs Education.
European Agency for Special Needs and Inclusive Education (2017). *Finland – Special Needs Education Within the Education System.* Available at: www.european-agency.org/country-information/finland/national-overview/special-needs-education-within-the-education-system [accessed on 03/08/2017].

European Agency for Special Needs and Inclusive Education (2017a). *Belgium (Flemish speaking community) – Financing.* Available at: https://www.european-agency.org/country-information/belgium-flemish-community/national-overview/financing [accessed on 03/09/2017].

European Commission/EACEA/Eurydice (2014). Financing Schools in Europe: Mechanisms, Methods and Criteria in Public Funding. Available at: http://eacea.ec.europa.eu/education/eurydice/documents/thematic_reports/170en.pdf. [accessed on 03/08/2017].

European Commission (2013). *Support for children with special educational needs (SEN).* Brussels: European Commission.

European Commission (2016). *Education and Training Monitor 2016 Estonia.* Available at: https://ec.europa.eu/education/sites/education/files/monitor2016-ee_en.pdf [accessed on 02/01/2018].

European Commission/EACEA/Eurydice (2017). Belgium (Flemish Community): *Special Education Needs Provision within Mainstream Education.* Available at: https://webgate.ec.europa.eu/fpfis/mwikis/eurydice/index.php/Belgium-Flemish-Community:Special_Education_Needs_Provision_within_Mainstream_Education [accessed on 01/09/2017].

Finnish National Agency for Education (2017). *Finnish Education in a Nutshell.* Helsinki: Grano Oy.

Finnish National Board of Education (n.d.). *TEACHERS IN FINLAND: Statistical Brochure.* Helsinki. Available at: https://www.oph.fi/download/166755_teachers_in_finland_statistical_brochure.pdf [accessed on 29/03/2019].

Finnish National Board of Education (2010). *Vocational education and training in Finland.* Helsinki.

Freeman, R. B., Machin, S., & Viarengo, M. (2010). *Variation in educational outcomes and policies across countries and of schools within countries* (No. w16293). National Bureau of Economic Research.

Garland, N. S. (2009). *Highly Capable Students Current: Programs in Washington and Other States.* Washington, DC.: Senate Committee Services.

Groenez S., Juchtmans G., Smet M., Stevens C. (2015). *Analyse van het nieuwe financieringsmechanisme voor de werkingsmiddelen van scholen.* Leuven: KU Leuven.

Guiltner N., McBride S. and M. Suddaby (2008). *Langley Special Education Inquiry Report. [state]* Langley SD#35.

Gustafson, C. (2012). *Public School Funding in Massachusetts: Where We Are, What Has Changed, and How We Compare to Other States.* Available at: http://massbudget.org/report_window.php?loc=ed_census_2012.html [accessed on 03/08/2017].

Hanushek, E. A., Link, S. & Woessmann, L. (2013). Does school autonomy make sense everywhere? Panel estimates from PISA. *Journal of Development Economics.* 104(C), p. 212-232.

Hanushek, E. A., and Woessmann, L. (2017). *School Resources and Student Achievement: A Review of Cross-Country Economic Research.* In Cognitive Abilities and Educational Outcomes. Springer International Publishing.

Hindriks, J., Verschelde, M., Rayp, G. and Schoors, K. (2010). *School autonomy and educational performance: within-country evidence.* No 2010082, CORE Discussion Papers, Université catholique de Louvain, Center for Operations Research and Econometrics (CORE).

Informatie Vlaanderen (2017a). *Compulsory education.* Flanders.be the official website of the Flemish government. Available at: http://www.flanders.be/en/studying/compulsory-education [accessed on 03/08/2017].

Informatie Vlaanderen (2017b). *Buitengewoon basisonderwijs.* Flanders.be the official website of the Flemish government. Available at: https://www.vlaanderen.be/nl/onderwijs-en-wetenschap/onderwijsaanbod/buitengewoon-basisonderwijs [accessed on 03/08/2017].

Informatie Vlaanderen (2017c). *Buitengewoon secundair onderwijs (BUSO).* Flanders.be the official website of the Flemish government. Available at: https://www.vlaanderen.be/nl/onderwijs-en-wetenschap/onderwijsaanbod/buitengewoon-secundair-onderwijs-buso [accessed on 03/08/2017].

REFERENCES

Jackson, C. K., Johnson, R. C., and Persico, C. (2016). *The effects of school spending on educational and economic outcomes: Evidence from school finance reforms*. Quarterly Journal of Economics, 131, 157-218.

Jensen B., Sonnemann, J., Roberts-Hull, K., and Hunter, A. (2016). *Beyond PD: Teacher Professional Learning in High-Performing Systems*. Washington, DC: National Center on Education and the Economy.

Jahnukainen, M. (2011). *Different Strategies, Different Outcomes? The History and Trends of the Inclusive and Special Education in Alberta (Canada) and in Finland*. Scandinavian Journal of Educational Research 55(5), 489–502.

King Rice, J. (2004). *Equity and efficiency in school finance reform: Competing or complementary goods?* Peabody Journal of Education, 79(3), 134–151.

Kirjavainen, T. (2010). *Esiselvitysraportti: Erityisopetuksen vaikuttavuus perusopetuksessa* [Report of the Preliminary Study: The Effectiveness of Special Education in Compulsory Education]. Helsinki: National Audit Office of Finland.

Kirjavainen, T., Pulkkinen, J., and Jahnukainen, M. (2014a). *Erityisoppilaiden osuuksien kuntakohtaiseen vaihteluun vaikuttaneet tekijät vuosina 2001–2010.* [Factors Affecting Municipal Variation in the Share of Students with Special Education Needs in 2001–2010]. Yhteiskuntapolitiikka 79 (6), 619–630.

Kirss, L. (2011). *Õppenõustamisteenustega rahulolu ja nende kättesaadavus*. Tallinn: Poliitikauuringute Keskus PRAXIS.

Levačić, R. (2011). *Per capita financing of education in Estonia*, in *Reforming Education Finance in Six Transition Countries: Six Case Studies in Per Capita Financing Systems*, Chapter 3, ed. By J.D Alonso and A. Sanchez, The World Bank, Washington, DC, http://elibrary.worldbank.org/doi/abs/10.1596/ 978-0-8213-8783-2#.

Luginbuhl, R., Webbink, D., and de Wolf, I. (2009). *Do inspections improve primary school performance?* Educational Evaluation and Policy Analysis, 31(3), 221–237.

Massachusetts Department of Elementary and Secondary Education (2017). *Enrollment Data (2016-17)*. Available at: http://profiles.doe.mass.edu/profiles/student.aspx?orgcode=00000000&orgtypecode=0&leftNavId=300& [accessed on 07/08/2017] MA, Boston: Malden.

Massachusetts Department of Elementary and Secondary Education (2017a). *The Massachusetts Foundation Budget*. Available at: http://www.doe.mass.edu/finance/chapter70/chapter-cal.pdf [accessed on 07/08/2017] MA: Malden.

MassBudget.org (2010). *Demystifying the Chapter 70 Formula: How the Massachusetts Education Funding System Works*. Available at http://www.massbudget.org/report_window.php?loc=Facts_10_22_10.html [accessed on 02/11/2017].

Matthews, P. and Sammons, P. (2004) *Improvement through Inspection: An Evaluation of the Impact of Ofsted's Work*. London: Ofsted.

McCrone, T., Coghlan, M., Wade, P. and Rudd, P. (2009). *Evaluation of the impact of section 5 inspections – Strand 3*. Final report for Ofsted.

McGrath, S. (1993). *Equity and efficiency in educational finance: An operational conundrum*. Available at: http://www.mun.ca/educ/faculty/mwatch/vol1/mcgrath2.html [accessed on 07/08/2017].

McLoughlin, J. A., and Lewis, R. B. (2008). *Assessing Students with Special Needs*. 7th ed. Columbus, OH: Pearson.

Ministry of Education and Research (2015). *OECD Review of Policies to Improve the Effectiveness of Resource Use in Schools: Country Background Report for Estonia*, Tartu. Available at: http://www.oecd.org/education/schoolresourcesreview.htm.

Minter, C. and Hoxby, C. M. (1996). *Are Efficiency and Equity in School Finance Substitutes or Complements?* The Journal of Economic Perspectives, 10(4), 51–72.

Nusche, D., et al. (2015). *OECD Reviews of School Resources: Flemish Community of Belgium 2015*. OECD Reviews of School Resources. OECD Publishing: Paris.

OECD (2011). *Estonia: Towards a Single Government Approach*. OECD Public Governance Reviews. Paris: OECD Publishing.
OECD (2013). *School Governance, Assessments and Accountability*. Paris: OECD Publishing.
OECD (2014). *PISA 2012 Results in Focus*. Paris: OECD Publishing.
OECD (2015). *Education Policy Outlook: Canada*. OECD Public Governance Reviews. Paris: OECD Publishing.
OECD (2015a). *Education Policy Outlook: Estonia*. OECD Public Governance Reviews. Paris: OECD Publishing.
OECD (2015b). *Education Policy Outlook: Finland*. OECD Public Governance Reviews. Paris: OECD Publishing.
OECD (2015c). *Estonia: PISA 2015 Higher Performers*. OECD Public Governance Reviews. Paris: OECD Publishing.
OECD (2015d). *Massachusetts: PISA 2015 Country Note*. OECD Public Governance Reviews. Paris: OECD Publishing.
OECD (2016). *Education at a Glance 2016: OECD Indicators*. Paris: OECD Publishing.
OECD (2016a). *PISA 2015 Results in Focus*. Paris: OECD Publishing.
OECD (2017). *Program for International Student Assessment (PISA), 2015 Reading, Mathematics and Science Assessment*. Available at: http://pisadataexplorer.oecd.org/ide/idepisa/ [accessed on 12/08/2017].
OECD (2019). *Young population (indicator)*. Available at: 10.1787/3d774f19-en [accessed on 28/03/19]
Official Statistics of Finland (2017). *Educational finances* [e-publication]. ISSN=1799-0963. 2015. Helsinki: Statistics Finland. Available at: http://www.stat.fi/til/kotal/2015/kotal_2015_2017-05-11_tie_001_en.html [accessed on 07/08/2017]
Official Statistics of Finland (2017a). *Providers of education and educational institutions* [e-publication]. ISSN=1799-5825. Helsinki: Statistics Finland. Available at: http://www.stat.fi/til/kjarj/index_en.html [accessed on 28/08/2017]
Okun, A. M. (1975). *Equality and Efficiency: The Big Tradeoff*. Washington, DC: Brookings Institution.
Padrik, M. (2010). *Word-formation skill in Estonian children with specific language impairment*. Tartu: Tartu University Press.
Province of British Columbia (2017). *K-12 Funding – Special Needs*. Available at: http://www2.gov.bc.ca/gov/content/education-training/administration/legislation-policy/public-schools/k-12-funding-special-needs [accessed on 07/08/2017]
RiigiTeataja.ee (2017). *Valdade ja linnade üldhariduskoolide toetuse arvestamise aluseks olevad koefitsiendid*. Available at: https://www.riigiteataja.ee/aktilisa/1050/7201/7020/VV_16m_lisa1.pdf [accessed on 07/08/2017]
Ross, K., and Levačić, R. (eds) (1999) *Needs Based Resource Allocation in Education via Formula Funding of Schools*, Paris, International Institute of Educational Planning.
Sahlberg, P. (2011). *Finnish Lessons. What Can the World Learn from Educational Change in Finland?* New York: Teachers College Press.
Santiago, P., et al. (2016). *OECD Reviews of School Resources: Estonia 2016*. OECD Reviews of School Resources. Paris: OECD Publishing.
Sherlock, T., and Skelton, C. (2005). *Gifted students not being identified in B.C.* Vancouver Sun. Available at http://www.vancouversun.com/g00/health/Gifted+students+being+identified/10698076/story.html [accessed on 03/08/2017].
Siegel, L., and Stewart, L. (2000). *A Review of Special Education in British Columbia*. British Columbia: Ministry of Education.

Statistics Estonia (2017a). *Minifacts about Estonia*. Available at http://www.stat.ee/publication-download-pdf?publication_id=44619 [accessed on 03/08/2017].
Statistics Estonia (2017b). *Eesti Statistika Kvartalikiri. 2/17. Quarterly Bulletin of Statistics Estonia.* Available at http://www.stat.ee/publication-download-pdf?publication_id=44111 [accessed on 03/08/2017].
Statistics Canada (2016a). *Table B.1.1.2 Annual expenditure by educational institutions per student, for all services, by educational level, in equivalent US dollars converted using purchasing power parity, Canada, provinces and territories, 2013/2014.* Available at http://www.statcan.gc.ca/pub/81-604-x/2016001/t/tblb1.1.2-eng.htm [accessed on 08/08/2017].
Statistics Canada (2016b). *Table B.2.1 Public and private expenditure on educational institutions as a percentage of GDP, by level of education, Canada, provinces and territories, 2013.* Available at http://www.statcan.gc.ca/pub/81-604-x/2016001/t/tblb2.1-eng.htm [accessed on 08/08/2017].
The Assembly Higher Education Committee (2003). *Summary of the Strengths & Weaknesses of the Existing Community College Funding Mechanism.* CA: Sacramento.
Tirri, K. and Kuusisto, E. (2013). *How Finland Serves Gifted and Talented Pupils.* Journal for the Education of the Gifted, 36(1), 84 – 96.
Toutkoushian, R., and Michael, R. (2007). *An alternative approach to measuring horizontal and vertical equity in school funding.* The Journal of Education Finance, 32, 395-421.
United Nations. (2006). *Convention on the Rights of Persons with Disabilities.* New York: United Nations.
Vaughn, S., and Denton, C. A. (2008). The Role of Intervention. In *Response to Intervention: A Framework for Reading Educators*, ed. by D. Fuchs, L. S. Fuchs and S. Vaughn, 51–70. Newark, DE: International Reading Association.
Verstegen, D. A. (2015). *A Quick Glance at School Finance: A 50 State Survey of School Finance Policies.* Available at https://schoolfinancesdav.wordpress.com/ [accessed on 08/03/2019].
Vlaamse Overheid. (1997). *Decreet basisonderwijs.* Brussels: Vlaamse Overheid.
Vlaamse Overheid. (1998). *Het werkingsbudget in het basisonderwijs.* Brussels: Vlaamse Overheid.
Vlaamse Overheid. (2005). *Personeelsformatie Scholen in het Gewoon Basisonderwijs.* Brussels: Vlaamse Overheid.
Vlaamse Overheid. (2014). *Beperking van het aantal uren die geen lesuren zijn en georganiseerd worden als bijzondere pedagogische taken in het secundair onderwijs.* Brussels: Vlaamse Overheid.
Vlaamse Overheid. (2016). *Vlaams onderwijs in cijfers 2015-2016 Basisonderwijs.* Brussels: Vlaamse Overheid.
Vlaamse Overheid. (2017). *Het ondersteuningsmodel in het basis- en secundair onderwijs en in het hoger onderwijs.* Brussels: Vlaamse Overheid.
Wuttke, J. (2007). Uncertainty and Bias in PISA. In *PISA ACCORDING TO PISA. DOES PISA KEEP WHAT IT PROMISES*, ed. by Hopmann, Brinek, Retzl, 241-263, Vienna.
Wößmann, L. (2008). *Efficiency and equity of European education and training policies.* International Tax and Public Finance, 15(2), 199–230.

CPSIA information can be obtained
at www.ICGtesting.com
Printed in the USA
LVHW082135041219
639438LV00003B/21/P